Exploring Materials

Creative Design for Everyday Objects

Inna Alesina and Ellen Lupton

PRINCETON ARCHITECTURAL PRESS, NEW YORK

MARYLAND INSTITUTE COLLEGE OF ART, BALTIMORE

Published by
Princeton Architectural Press
37 East Seventh Street
New York, New York 10003

For a free catalog of books, call 1.800.722.6657.
Visit our website at www.papress.com.

Editing: Clare Jacobson
Editorial assistance: Carolyn Deuschle
Book design: Inna Alesina, Justin Kropp, and Ellen Lupton
Cover design: Julia Kostreva, Inna Alesina, and Ellen Lupton
Photography: Inna Alesina (unless noted otherwise)
Typography: Thesis, designed by Lucas de Groot

Special thanks to: Nettie Aljian, Bree Anne Apperley, Sara Bader,
Nicola Bednarek, Janet Behning, Becca Casbon, Carina Cha,
Tom Cho, Penny (Yuen Pik) Chu, Russell Fernandez, Pete Fitzpatrick,
Wendy Fuller, Jan Haux, Linda Lee, Laurie Manfra, John Myers,
Katharine Myers, Daniel Simon, Andrew Stepanian, Jennifer
Thompson, Paul Wagner, Joseph Weston, and Deb Wood of
Princeton Architectural Press
—Kevin C. Lippert, publisher

Library of Congress Cataloging-in-Publication Data
Alesina, Inna, 1969–
  Exploring materials : creative design for everyday objects / Inna
Alesina and Ellen Lupton. — 1st ed.
     p. cm.
  Includes bibliographical references and index.
 ISBN 978-1-56898-768-2 (alk. paper)
 1. Materials. 2. Design, Industrial. I. Lupton, Ellen. II. Title.
 TA403.6.A447 2009
 745.2—dc22
                                        2008032530

This publication is a project of
The Center for Design Thinking
Maryland Institute College of Art
1300 Mt. Royal Avenue
Baltimore, Maryland 21217
www.mica.edu

CONTENTS

INTRODUCTION: *How to Use This Book*

Designers can find unexpected solutions when they work with physical forms and materials in a direct, active, hands-on way. Sketching ideas with a pencil or rendering them with computer software are useful experiences, but there is no substitute for confronting physical materials in the flesh. Foam, mesh, wood, plastic, and wire each have behaviors and properties that suggest different types of structure, surface, and connection. In place of the abstraction of pure volumes or the whimsy of "virtual" objects, this book encourages designers to make and test real objects in a studio environment.

Materials are like words. The richer your design vocabulary, the more solutions you can see and express. There are no good or bad materials. Each one has its place, consequences, and cost. Understanding materials is essential to design. Some designers come to the profession with a commonsense knowledge of materials, while others have only thought about their decorative properties. Use this book to begin looking at materials with new eyes. Ignore what you already know, and find out how you can coax cardboard, foam, cloth, metal, or rope into surprising structures with valuable functions.

Our book is an invitation to get inspired by materials. One of our designer friends dislikes the term *inspired*. To him, to be inspired means to copy someone else's work. He thinks designers should use the phrase "based on research" instead. But when we say "inspired by materials," we do not mean following the form of an existing object. We mean studying the properties and behavior of a physical substance to discover and invent forms and solutions.

Exploring Materials is a book for students, designers, artists, and anyone interested in making objects. The first chapter lays out our approach with a case study drawn from a classroom project. A group of designers was asked to solve a common problem (an object for sitting) using a particular material. Instead of beginning with an end result in

PRODUCT DESIGN IS PHYSICAL. ENGAGING WITH REAL MATERIALS AND REAL TOOLS IS AN ESSENTIAL
ASPECT OF DESIGN THINKING. HOW DO MATERIALS BEHAVE? HOW DO THEY FEEL TO THE HAND AND BODY?

mind, each designer explored the material at hand—foam, felt, wire, and so on. The solutions are as different as the substances. The projects are rough and unrefined, but each one departs from the ordinary.

The second chapter uses another classroom experiment to explore the design process in more detail. Here, a team of designers thought about creating an alternative to the standard shopping bag. Their research involved brainstorming, observing consumers and workers, and experiencing the act of shopping in a critical way. They made hands-on prototypes and tested them in real environments.

At the core of our book is a visual glossary of thirty-four materials, organized both to inspire and to inform. Although most of these materials are commonplace (rather than "smart" substances or exotic mutants), each is packed with potential ideas. This section presents everyday uses of the materials, pointing out the special ways each one functions as a structure, surface, fastener, and more. Also featured are experimental uses of these forms and substances, showing how designers from around the world have exploited their characteristics in inventive ways. The book concludes with a section on making it real, moving beyond the prototype to create a product that can be manufactured and marketed.

Exploring Materials speaks to a cultural shift in the design world. Many designers are thinking critically and creatively about materials— about where they come from, how they function, and where they end up at the end of a product's life cycle. There is growing interest across society in physically making things and thus directly engaging with objects and the environment. The revitalization of craft has helped revitalize design. This book embraces this new wave of thinking and making. We hope you will use it stimulate your own mind and to make your own ideas real.— *Inna Alesina and Ellen Lupton*

OPEN MIND. In response to the challenge to make a sitting structure with yarn, the designers created a new and unfamiliar object. Design: Maria Duke, MICA.

UNLOCK IDEAS

USING MATERIALS FOR INSPIRATION

The projects shown on the following pages were created by design students at Maryland Institute College of Art (MICA). The goal of these experiments was to unlock creativity by exploring the unique properties of materials. Whereas traditional design methodologies focus on sketching, our approach emphasizes hands-on prototyping with three-dimensional structures. Thus the works shown here are not slick finished products (or glossy 3D renderings of slick finished products). Instead they are active, raw projects produced with real materials and real tools in a studio environment.

To initiate these experiments, we asked a group of design students to address a particular challenge: make a person comfortable while sitting. Naturally, each designer immediately began thinking about chairs. Then we asked them to put aside their ideas about chairs and focus instead on a particular material (foam, rope, wire, cardboard, metal rods, etc.). The designers explored each material, uncovering its properties as a surface, structure, and fastener. They could not rely on what they already knew about chairs: legs, back, seat, arms, and so on. By exploring materials rather than pursuing a preconceived end product, these designers began thinking in new ways.

The best way to learn is by doing. In the exercises documented here, designers stated a challenge and then solved it with a randomly assigned material. Try it yourself and see what ideas emerge. Then, change materials and try it again. See how your results are different. This exercise is a kind of game. It is also a tool for inventing, brainstorming, and generating ideas. You can apply it to any type of challenge—not just creating an object but planning a process, studying a system, or designing a space. Kids, artists, designers, and even business people can broaden their thinking with this technique.

EXPLORING MOLDED FOAM

In the experimental project shown here, the challenge was to use molded foam to make a structure for sitting. Thus the project did not focus on "designing a chair" as an end result; instead, it focused on understanding sitting, comfort, and shape in a broader way.

It sounds easy to design a chair with foam, as this material is already associated with comfort and padding. However, the unique properties of molded foam can inspire surprising solutions.

Foam comes in many forms. Urethane foam sheets are used for traditional padding and upholstery. Closed-cell foams like Styrofoam insulation and polyethylene-extruded shapes are used for packing and flotation.

We used sheets of high-density urethane foam to create an object that transforms from an upright to a horizontal position, supporting either a seated or a reclining body.

TRANSFORMABLE OBJECTS. The North Tiles is a transformable object made from fabric-covered foam sheets. Design: Ronan and Erwan Bouroullec

AVAILABLE MATERIALS. We used readily available products like carpeting foam and packing materials to test ideas. How much structure is enough? Can we use other objects like walls or pillars to help us? Foam experiments by Cecilia Oh, MICA.

MOCK-UPS. In this design, modular geometric shapes contrast with the softness of foam. We used small paper models for quick prototyping. Making cardboard mock-ups at actual scale helped establish dimensions and uncover overall structural issues. The volume shown here is hollow. To be useful as a seat, each triangle needed to become a base for a solid truncated tetrahedron.

FOAM CHAIR/SLIPPER. The object is designed to transform with use. It can be used for sitting during the day and lying down at night. When put back into a chair, the tetrahedrons fit inside like pieces in a puzzle. Design: Haiji Park, MICA.

EXPLORING YARN

Here, the challenge was to use yarn as a primary material in a sitting object. An obvious approach would have been to use skeins of yarn as stuffing and padding. Instead, we created surfaces and fasteners with yarn. Inspired by the craft of embroidering with a round tambour or hoop, we hand-embroidered the yarn around a welded metal frame to create a transparent rocker. Square steel mesh was attached to the welded frame to create an embroidery surface, similar to the plastic canvas used for needlepoint. Users can sit inside the hoop and add embroidery.

YARN AND METAL CHAIR. Making small-scale models is important to the thought process. Thanks to the round shape, the prototype can be easily transported to the studio from the metal shop. Embroidery details can be added to the surface by someone relaxing in the chair. Design: Maria Duke, MICA.

EXPLORING ROPE

How can rope be used to make a chair? To create the object shown here, we studied knots and knotting techniques. We created a minimal metal frame, welded from metal rods, to support the rope structure. The resulting object is light, both physically and visually.

To quickly test the welded structure, we wrapped it tightly with ordinary plastic wrap. Several problems emerged during the testing process, including the bending of the structure under weight. So we went back to the welding shop to add more structure.

ROPE AND METAL CHAIR. We resolved the issue of the rope slipping along the metal frame by wrapping rope around the metal rod to create spacers between the knots. Design: Lily Worledge, MICA.

EXPLORING FELT

Industrial felt is a nonwoven textile that comes in sheets. It is easy to cut, fold, and fasten. Here, the challenge was to use this soft, flexible material in a structural way to support the human body.

Rolling the felt into cylinders yielded strong building elements. Industrial felt is available in a variety of densities; the denser the fibers, the more expensive the material. To keep costs down while using a lower-density felt, we reinforced the bottom parts of some of the rolls with cardboard.

The entire structure is fastened together with webbing straps. The piece can be taken apart to be turned into a series of blankets or to be cleaned.

FELT CHAIR. Buckled webbing keeps the parts of the chair together. Books and magazines can be stored between the chair's outer layers. Design: Huei-Ting Wu, MICA.

EXPLORING CORRUGATED CARDBOARD

Designers have experimented with corrugated cardboard as a material for decades, using this material to make inexpensive, lightweight furniture. In the prototype shown here, we created a honeycomb structure and carved out a space for the body. The whole structure is secured with industrial plastic straps.

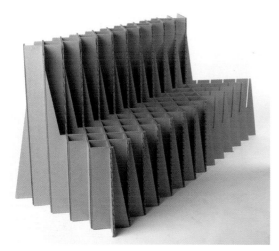

EXBOX BENCH. This cardboard lattice bench consists of potentially infinite numbers of sheets slotted together to form a collapsible seating arrangement. Design: Giles Miller.

CARDBOARD CHAIR. Found throughout nature, honeycomb structures are strong and light. Our cardboard chair is easy to move. Design: Hyeshin Kim, MICA.

EXPLORING WIRE

Wire springs are hidden inside many common furnishings, including mattresses and couches. The donut-shaped chair shown here is inspired by springs and coiled wire. A continuous ribbon of fabric is woven through the wire, helping control the material as well as creating a soft outer surface. The structure folds for portability.

WIRE CHAIR. The completed prototype is tested for comfort and folding. Design: Whitney Campbell, MICA.

EXPLORING METAL ROD

Metal rods are similar to wire, but they are more structural and therefore lend themselves more easily to the problem of supporting the human body. Almost invisible, the object shown here could be used outdoors as well as indoors. If placed in a garden, it would cast almost no shadow, allowing plants and grasses to grow through it. The object is sculptural as well as functional.

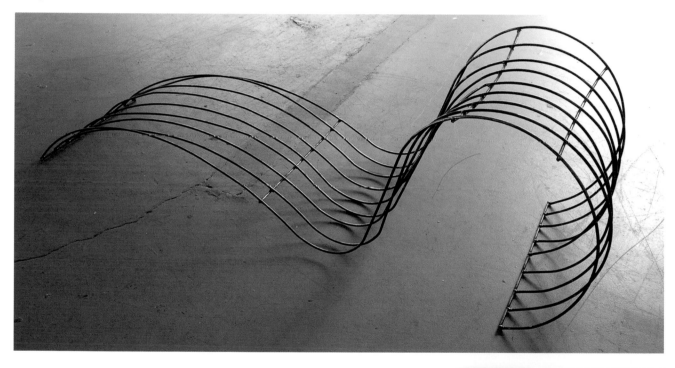

INVISIBLE FORM. The structure is light, physically and visually. Design: Samantha Pasapane, MICA.

EXPLORING RUBBER

How can rubber become a chair? Rubber is formed through many processes, including dipping, molding, and inflating. The experiment shown here is made from recycled bike inner tubes. By stitching cut inner tubes together, we created a durable yet elastic sack. When stuffed with clothes while traveling, the object can be used as a place for sitting, resting, and reclining against walls.

RUBBER CHAIR. Old inner tubes were salvaged from a local bike shop—an excellent source of free rubber. The piece serves as a backpack or a wearable storage unit as well as a chair (similar to a bean bag) or as a place to sleep. Design: Katie Coble, MICA.

EXPLORING PLYWOOD

Plywood has many uses in furniture making. Explored here is the idea of a see-through structure that can be shipped flat and assembled by the user. The empty spaces inside this reading chair can be used for storing books and magazines. The pieces left over from the production process could be made into complementary objects such as bookshelves and light fixtures.

PLYWOOD CHAIR. The cut elements are designed to notch together without glue. The finished chair resembles an open skeleton. Design: Irina Dukhnevich, MICA.

Plastic bags are cheap and useful—and an environmental hazard. How do different users see them?

CUSTOMER: Plastic bags help make shopping with small children less stressful. It is easier to shove everything into bags and out of sight; otherwise, kids grab and eat unwashed stuff. Some fruit boxes are sprayed with chemicals that are not safe for kids, and so they are not a good alternative to bags. When moving groceries from the cart to the car, it's useful to be able to see what's inside the bags. Did I buy what I needed? Did I buy too much? Will this spoil before I get home? Can something tip over and break in the car?

MANAGER: Speedy checkout and happy customers are top priorities. Reusable bags take more time for cashiers. Free bags are part of the culture in the U.S., and it is hard to challenge this custom. Will customers be angry if they don't get free bags? Will cashiers get frustrated explaining a new policy? When we tried to eliminate plastic bags altogether in one store, the cashiers had a problem with it. Shopping bags are also a security device; they provide one of the easiest ways for us to see if items were paid for, preventing theft.

FARMER: What kind of packaging is needed to get crops safely to the store? How can I ensure my product looks presentable when displayed? How will people recognize my brand? How can I make it easy for people to purchase fresh produce? Plastic bags address all of these questions.

STUDY, PROTOTYPE, TEST

JOURNEY THROUGH THE DESIGN PROCESS

The case study laid out in the following pages follows a team of design students at Maryland Institute College of Art who set out to invent a better shopping bag. They focused on what people need when shopping for produce and fresh food. They brainstormed, considered the viewpoints of different users, explored multiple design directions, constructed prototypes, and tested their prototypes. Putting aside given expectations about what a shopping bag should be, they came up with unexpected solutions. The experimental concepts they developed and the thought process they pursued could inspire you to study and solve this challenge yourself—and others like it.

Plastic bags are not really recyclable. The chasing arrows symbol makes people feel better about using them, but plastic bags can't be recycled with other household items in many areas. Some bags get down-cycled into plastic lumber, whose next stop is the landfill. Plastic bags are not biodegradable in a conventional landfill, because they need air and light to decompose, and even then they don't give nutrients to the earth—they just break down into smaller bits of plastic. They are also a hazard to wildlife.

Can we solve the challenge solely with design? Maybe a new service or government regulation is required, not a new product. Stores could be the first to resist new ideas about shopping bags. Will a new system make people buy less stuff? What about eliminating the store altogether through community-supported agriculture or cooperative shopping?

This chapter shows how to turn your observations of everyday life into useful and original ideas. Get in the mood for creative problem-solving by discovering design concepts and design challenges all around you. As designers we need to ask ourselves, "How can we create something meaningful that makes people's lives easier, safer, and more pleasurable, and doesn't damage the environment?"

IDENTIFY THE PROBLEM

Why is it so important to find the right problem to solve? It is a basic human desire to come up with solutions in response to a challenge. Solutions are valued; we are judged by the results. However, it is a mistake to jump into solutions at the outset of a project. Learn how to step back and see the big picture. Rather than focus on designing a shopping bag, we will try to broaden our thinking to consider other possible solutions. State your design problem in a way that opens up possibilities for multiple design solutions.

LIMITED THINKING. If a designer is asked to create a shopping bag, he or she will use design thinking and will be able to create a better shopping bag. Our approach is different. By not defining the solution at the outset, we are not limiting our thinking to certain kinds of products. The final outcome may be a new and different bag, but we will explore other possibilities along the way.

CHALLENGE:
Think of ways to get groceries from the store to the consumer's home

OPEN-ENDED THINKING. State the basic challenge in broad rather than narrow terms. Think about solutions that aren't yet known. The problem doesn't presume the nature of the solution.

MULTIPLE DIRECTIONS. There are many ways to take groceries home: in a bag, on your back, on your head. Each direction has pros and cons. At this stage, we are not judging solutions but rather widening the scope of our problem.

WHAT ARE YOU TRYING TO ACHIEVE? WRITE DOWN AND PRIORITIZE YOUR DESIGN GOALS. ONCE YOU HAVE ESTABLISHED A PERSPECTIVE, YOU CAN DIG DEEPER INTO EACH SUBJECT.

USER PERSPECTIVE

Create a better shopping experience.

BUSINESS PERSPECTIVE

Make it economical.

ENVIRONMENTAL PERSPECTIVE

Minimize waste.

This part of our thinking will focus on the customer. A better shopping experience will mean different things to different people.

For our solution to work, it has to make economic sense for the farmer, the store, and the customer.

Everything has an impact on the environment, from the kinds of crops grown and agricultural techniques used to transportation, consumption, and disposal.

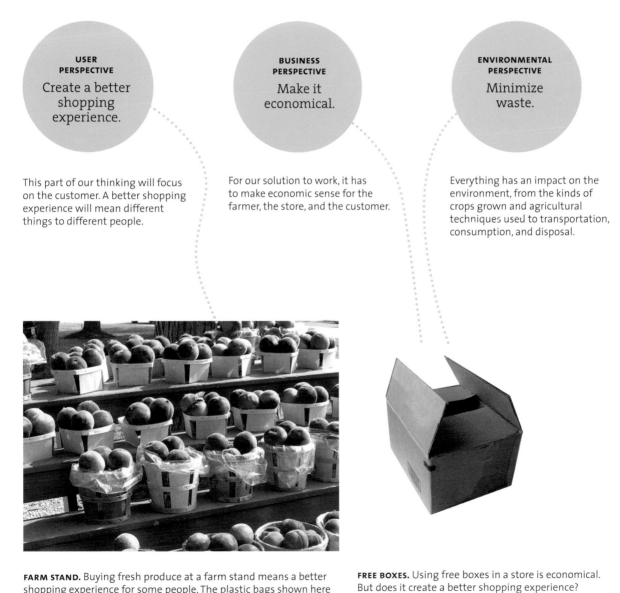

FARM STAND. Buying fresh produce at a farm stand means a better shopping experience for some people. The plastic bags shown here are both easy to carry by the consumer and easy on the farmer to sell, since customers will not inspect every single peach in the bag. This solution is efficient, safe, and durable. But is it good for the environment?

FREE BOXES. Using free boxes in a store is economical. But does it create a better shopping experience?

WIDEN THE PROBLEM

Having set forth the basic goals that will inform our work, now it is time to brainstorm. Remember, we do not start our thinking with existing solutions, so why should we stop at obvious problems? Here, we hypothesize what the problems are; we will have a chance to research these issues later. For now, we keep widening the problem. Our goal is to find interesting challenges to solve. Thus when we visit stores to research and observe, we will already have a list of questions to ask. This will help us weed out bad ideas quickly.

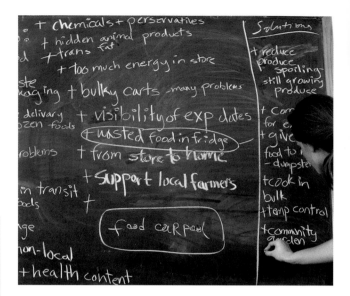

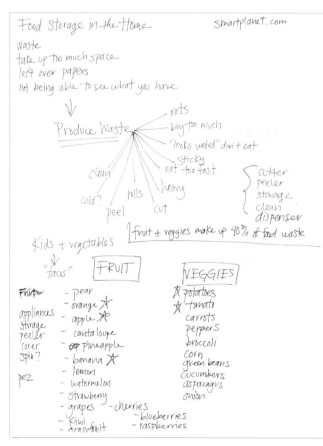

MAKE A LIST. We listed all the challenges we could think of about delivering food from the farmer to the end consumer. Looking beyond the bag took us in unexpected directions.

Brainstorming works best as a team exercise.

Focus on quantity. The greater the number of ideas generated, the greater the chance of producing a new and effective solution.

Avoid criticism. In a group brainstorming session, criticism should be put on hold. Instead of immediately stating what might be wrong with an idea, the participants focus on extending or adding to it, reserving analysis for a later stage of the process.

Welcome unusual ideas. To produce a long, rich list of ideas, include any strange or improbable proposal in your brainstorming process. These oddball concepts may open up new ways of thinking. Unusual ideas can be generated by looking at the challenge from another perspective or setting aside assumptions.

Combine and improve ideas. Several ideas can be combined to form a stronger single good idea. Use the process of association to arrive at more comprehensive concepts.

Limit the time. Participants in group brainstorming will stay more creative and avoid fatigue when there is a limit on time. Try one minute per problem.

Document every idea. Once you have listed all the problems the team can think of, pick each problem in turn and imagine possible solutions. This process can be done in words, sketches, or mock-ups.

TO UNDERSTAND OUR CHALLENGE BETTER WE CREATED SCENARIOS. THE SCENARIO CAN BECOME THE BASIS FOR DEVELOPING OTHER OUTCOMES AND FOR VISUALIZING DESIGN SOLUTIONS. HOW WILL OUR SOLUTION FUNCTION, AND WHAT WILL IT LOOK LIKE? WHAT INFRASTRUCTURE WILL ARISE TO SUPPORT IT?

As we brainstorm, possible scenarios are already popping into our minds. The best way to capture those ideas is to do a short session that looks at both problems and possible solutions. Explore outlandish "blue sky" ideas as well as more obvious directions. These scenarios may inspire feasible ideas later. At this stage, we are not designing a particular product (a bag); instead, we are talking about wider scenarios of how people might shop in the future. We are talking about how behaviors can change and then about possible technologies, materials, and products that will be needed to make this change happen. The solution will probably be a system rather than a product, involving components such as infrastructure, communication networks, materials, and laws.

Problems, problems, more problems.

At this stage, we are looking for problems, not solutions.

For example, we all know that a lot of produce is wasted along the way from farmer to consumer (an average of $300 worth of produce per day, per supermarket). Did you know that most of this wasted produce is spoiled from consumers touching it? Thus we can add another challenge to our list: How can our delivery system help prevent groceries from spoiling?

Did you know that 50 percent of the energy used by supermarkets is wasted by the refrigerators and freezers? While open refrigerator cases are user-friendly, they are especially wasteful. Some grocery stores actually turn on the heat in the summer to compensate for the cold air coming off the refrigerator cases.

MEALS ON WHEELS. Some items could be dispensed from a vending machine. How about creating milk, juice, and egg packaging with integrated "wheels" for gravity-assisted dispensing? Maybe you could load items directly into your car with no need for a bag. Concept: Manya Caralle and Caylan Weisel, MICA.

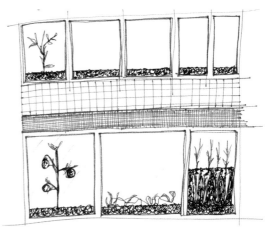

GREENHOUSE KITCHEN. What if food could continue to grow in my kitchen? What if the bag became a medium for food to grow in, or, better yet, the bag was designed to become the "soil" that keeps produce staying fresh at home? What if my kitchen could become a "food factory," so I would go to the store to get ingredients but would bake my own bread, eliminating over packaged goods? We went through a lot of blue sky ideas like these to "think outside the bag." Concept: Andrea Dombrowski, MICA.

IMAGINE SCENARIOS

Our design team thought about different ways that groceries could be produced and distributed in the future. Today, most shopping in the U.S. looks like it did in the 1950s: people drive their cars to the supermarket and bring home goods wrapped in disposable packaging. What if people could order their groceries online and have them delivered directly to their homes and neighborhoods instead? What if vacant lots and abandoned big-box stores were reborn as local farms? Imagining scenarios like these helps inspire designers to come up with new uses for familiar objects, spaces, and services. Sketches and Photoshop montages provide a quick way to visualize ideas.

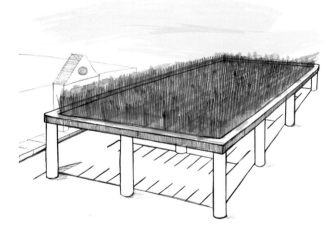

MASS TRANSIT FOR FOOD. Vans, trains, school buses, and postal trucks could be used to distribute groceries, bringing food to homes and neighborhoods. A train could be outfitted as a mobile farmers' market, traveling through neighborhoods with local produce. School buses that typically sit idle during the day could drop off food to homes and apartment buildings. Design: Sunny Chong, Geoff Kfoury, Louise Markison, Keloni Parks, and Stephanie Sevich, MICA.

GREEN ROOFS. Today, open parking lots create runoff and pollution and are expensive to illuminate at night. In contrast, covered parking structures with green roofs could provide produce for sale in greenhouse-equipped farming markets. The parking structures would reduce runoff and require less electricity to operate. Design: Kristian Bjornard, MICA.

ABANDONED LOTS ARE A BLIGHT ON MANY AMERICAN CITIES. GREENING THESE OPEN SPACES WOULD CREATE AN ECONOMIC AND CULTURAL RESOURCE.

food from urban garden

biowaste, manure, animal
bedding, newspapers,
compostables

methane

fertilizer

biodigester

oven stove,
electric generator

hot meal

SUSTAINABLE URBAN FARM/KITCHEN

URBAN FARM AND KITCHEN. An inner-city lot could become an energy-efficient community farm. Goats and chickens would provide food for people and organic waste for a methane biodigester, which anaerobically converts waste into biogas for the stove and fertilizer for the garden. With eggs, goat milk, produce, and a working stovetop, a meal could be made in the urban outdoors. Design: Virginia Sasser, MICA.

1. goats
2. chicken coop
3. kitchen
4. rooftop plants
5. farmers
6. methane biodigester
7. vegetable garden boxes
8. plant overhang / leisure area
9. gutter to flow water into biodigester

FIELD RESEARCH

We visited stores, talking to managers and shoppers and documenting the physical environment of each store. We learned about issues by actively observing people in the store—and by shopping ourselves. We tried to understand how and why things are done in the real world. We became users. Companies spend a lot of money to do consumer research. Working informally, we too gathered some valuable information.

Some designers visit users in their homes and videotape them. Often, you can learn something about people's behaviors and preferences by watching the video later—you'll notice details that you weren't focused on at the time. Taking notes and photographs during any research trip is always helpful. Don't count on yourself to remember your observations later.

Prepare for your research trip

Find out driving directions.

Pack camera, camcorder, notebook, and pen.

Make a list of questions.

Visit store at the least busy time to ensure that the manager has time to talk to you.

Make an appointment in advance if possible.

ROUGH EDGES. The serrated edge on paper grocery bags prevents paper cuts, which can be a problem with paper bags.

EXISTING SOLUTIONS. Some stores collect bags for recycling, but this is really a down-cycling of the plastic into less-valuable resources.

GET OUTSIDE THE STUDIO, TALK TO PEOPLE, BECOME A USER.

LISTEN. Interview with a store manager at a local grocery store in Baltimore.

Interview with manager at a home-furnishing store:

DESIGNER: Do you offer customers a choice regarding how their purchases are packed?

MANAGER: We are eliminating free disposable plastic bags altogether. We offer reusable bags for sale and free boxes for customers to reuse.

DESIGNER: What do you think about the current plastic bag issue?

MANAGER: As we get rid of free plastic bags, some customers will be shocked. But our store has always surprised shoppers. I hope the customers will come back even though they won't get a free bag.

DESIGNER: Would an education campaign help explain why you are doing this?

MANAGER: That might be a good idea. We have always used graphics in our store to explain our merchandise and point of view, so why not?

Interview with manager at a big-box store.

DESIGNER: Do you offer customers greener alternatives to a shopping bag?

MANAGER: Our goal is to make customers happy. If they want double bags, we will do that for them. Our corporation doesn't want to look "cheap," as if we are saving on bags.

DESIGNER: What do you think about the current plastic bag issue?

MANAGER: I don't have an opinion.

DESIGNER: How many bags do you use each day?

MANAGER: I can't tell you, but we use a lot of bags.

Interview with a customer at the same store.

DESIGNER: Would you bring your own bag to shop?

CUSTOMER: I would like to bring my own bag, but I feel it is inappropriate in this store.

DESIGNER: Do you have problems with plastic bags?

CUSTOMER: They break too easily. Also, the handle hurts my hands. But I hate when they double-bag everything. That's a wasteful solution.

BRAINSTORM WITH MATERIALS

Back to the drawing board. After getting a reality check from our shopping trips, we try not to get discouraged. An exercise that helps break away from the "everything has been done" block is to brainstorm with materials. This exercise is similar to the method described in the first chapter, where we used materials for inspiration. To use this sketching exercise, establish a simple challenge, such as how to carry groceries, and limit yourself to one material and see what kinds of solutions you can come up with. For example, an adhesive label will inspire different solutions for delivering produce than plastic mesh, an old T-shirt, or an inflatable structure will.

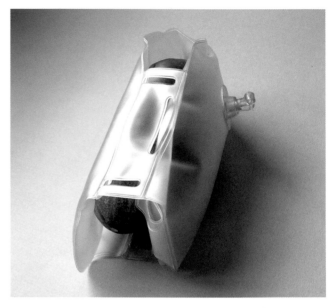

CUSHIONING WITH AIR. Here is an idea for a multiuse inflatable egg or fruit package. Air is a good insulator, keeping produce cold. In a one-shape-fits-all design, each cell will hold an apple or banana. When inflated, it will take the right shape.

MATERIALS LIBRARY. It is helpful to create your own library of inspiring materials. There are also companies such as Inventables, Material Connexion, and Materials Monthly that provide this service to designers. A subscription gets you information and physical samples of new and experimental materials.

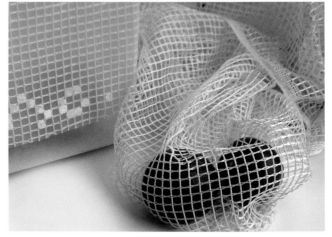

FREE SAMPLES. Many manufacturers are happy to provide designers with samples of their materials. Here, we got a sample of mesh from the manufacturer. It was enough material to make a mock-up of a potential solution.

DIFFERENT MATERIALS INSPIRE DIFFERENT SOLUTIONS. YOUR FIRST CONCEPTS DON'T HAVE TO BE REALISTIC. THINK OUTSIDE THE BAG!

Take the process a step further and work hands-on with ordinary yet unconventional materials, like plastic straws, soda bottles, string, and Bubble Wrap. This approach encourages creative thinking. It also helps you understand the structural properties of materials.

Any material can be used as a surface, a structure, or a fastener. Use items that you have on hand to try out different ideas in a direct, physical way. Try not to think about how you have seen the problem solved before. To make a first round of quick mock-ups, we used existing bags, food packaging, paper pulp trays, and even vertical window blinds. Being resourceful pays off, since supply costs add up.

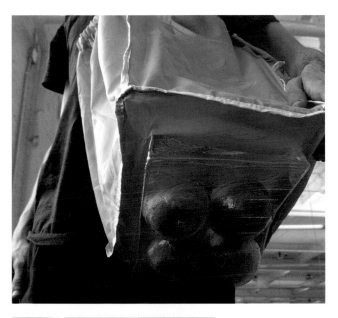

WORK WITH WHAT YOU HAVE. An old T-shirt was cut to make a stretchable sack. Design: Inna Alesina.

SEE-THROUGH MATERIALS. We brainstormed about a speedy check-out system where all the items would get scanned in a single sweep. We designed several bag prototypes with transparent materials for scanning in the bag. We realized that every kind of produce has its own shape, and you can't fit bananas into a shape made for oranges. Could universal shapes work? Concept: Benjamin Howard, MICA.

GET INSPIRED

Where do you get ideas? Given a problem, anyone can come up with a solution sooner or later. But how do you make it sooner? Ideas come to us in unlikely places. Some people are more likely to get an idea while taking a shower or taking a hike than sitting at a desk. Let's examine this process from our problem's point of view.

TRADITIONAL CRAFTS can show how people have used materials to solve problems in the past. For example, a basket made of woven palm leaves is a beautiful and efficient way to carry and store things.

PEOPLE. Observing people doing tasks gives us ideas about their behaviors. People might not realize that a problem exists, but watching them can expose problems. For example, kids want to participate in shopping; can we provide a way for them to do so?

NATURE is a good source for inspiration, since it has already solved countless problems many times over. Look at how nature has solved the problem of storing and transporting valuable things (seeds for future trees) by packing them closely together. Examples of nature-inspired designs include Velcro, the helicopter, and silk. This area of design is called biomimicry.

IF YOU GOOGLE "GROCERY BAG," YOU WILL SEE MANY EXISTING SOLUTIONS THAT CAN LIMIT YOUR THINKING. WE LOOKED AT PEOPLE, NATURE, TRADITIONAL CRAFTS, AND OBJECTS FROM OTHER CONTEXTS IN ORDER TO CREATE SOMETHING UNEXPECTED.

OBJECTS FROM OTHER CONTEXTS can have solutions relevant to your problem. For example, a tool belt could inspire a grocery carrier. Distributing weight makes the tools easy to carry.

EVERYDAY OBJECTS are a constant source of inspiration. Simple, disposable, inexpensive objects have often resulted from intense thinking by designers and engineers. Many have survived the test of time to become hidden classics of functional design—so commonplace, we fail to notice them. Take a close look at objects around you and analyze why they are made the way they are. Can you learn something from the way material is minimized in the structural properties of an egg carton? Apply the same thinking to your challenge.

Collect inspiring images and samples

Create an inspiration board to be visible when you are developing ideas. Collect images, objects, and materials.

Cut out magazine pictures to create a visual story about the end user.

Write key words describing the challenge. Cut and paste them on the board.

IN OTHER PARTS OF THE WORLD people could be solving your problem with materials that are readily available to them. This watermelon carrier is a minimal structure that allows one or two people to transport a heavy watermelon.

SKETCH

Sketching is an essential tool for visualizing concepts. Some designers use words and drawings interchangeably during the design process, making quick lists and simple drawings in a continuous cycle. In the first chapter, we recommend using an additional method for thinking with materials, working in 3D instead of 2D to generate ideas. Sketching, however, is the most convenient way to generate and communicate many ideas quickly. It is also useful for figuring out details. Sketching is a unique way to get ideas out of your head and to begin to make them understandable.

Some designers rush into making computer renderings before developing basic ideas on paper. Other designers become adept at making flashy, stylized product renderings with pencils and markers that produce sexy images more than solve problems. Some designers judge one another by the ability to make a pair of sneakers look like a sports car. Bottom line: being able to create beautiful sketches does not guarantee being able to solve problems elegantly. The ability to think and communicate with drawings, however, is an essential design skill.

DRAWINGS ARE AN IMPORTANT WAY TO LOOK AT DIFFERENT IDEAS QUICKLY. PIN THEM ON THE WALL TO ALLOW COMPARISONS AND TO SHARE IDEAS WITH YOUR TEAM. HERE ARE SOME SKETCHES THAT HELPED US VISUALIZE GROCERY BAG CONCEPTS.

Carry and Display

PROS. These objects encourage shoppers to experience food gathering as a precious activity. Ideas are derived from the way soft fruits are transported to the store or market in stackable boxes or baskets.

CONS. These objects need more space for storage. It takes time to carefully place fruits in compartments.

HOW IT WORKS. Each fruit is weighed at the stand. A sticker with a barcode is attached to the bag, so there is no need to remove the produce at the checkout. The same structure is used to wash and display fruits at home.

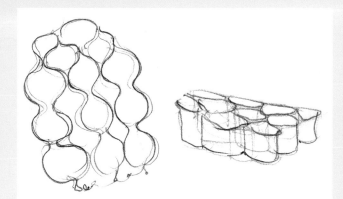

EGG CRATES provide a useful model.

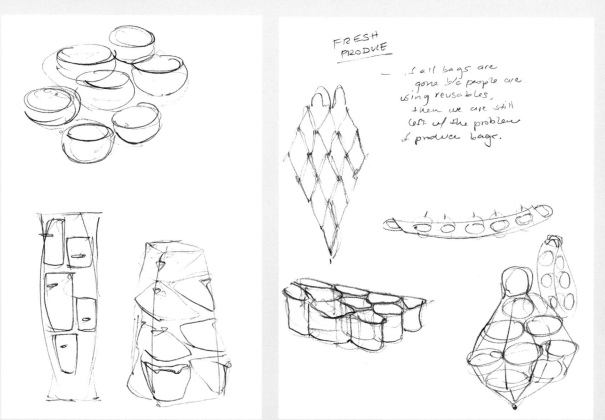

VERTICAL STRUCTURES get us thinking in another direction.

THINK ABOUT STRUCTURES that are stackable and compartmentalized.

PROTOTYPE AND TEST

After experiencing reality at the store and getting inspired by ideas from different industries and cultures, we were ready to focus on some practical solutions. We constructed working prototypes that we could test and refine. We started by carrying our prototypes around the studio, taking them in and out of the car, and taking them to stores. Getting feedback from store managers and consumers was valuable to our process.

Some issues arose that we didn't anticipate. One prototype was too big to fit on the checkout counter. Another made out of paper was too weak and had to be made of canvas instead. The canvas bag was handcrafted and would be difficult to mass-produce. We considered using grommets instead of stitches, or making the bag from plastic so that it would be commercially viable.

While working on our own solutions, we analyzed existing products from the same points of view we were using for our designs: environment, consumer, store manager, producer. What makes one design better than the others?

REUSING BOXES could save the store money on trash disposal. Although reusing boxes should be a win/win situation, it brings up many potential issues, including liability with regard to accidents or contamination.

FRANKENSTEIN PRODUCT. This container uses seven different materials plus two different printed surfaces. It is impossible to recycle. The wooden posts allow boxes to be stacked higher than cardboard containers.

COMPOSITE MATERIAL/NONRECYCLABLE. This package can't be recycled because it is made from a composite material with glossy printing. The box folds flat and has a carrying handle. This design provides a nice visual surprise.

SINGLE MATERIAL/RECYCLABLE. This package is made from one piece of folded cardboard, which is both recycled and recyclable. It has a carrying handle. The design is not very interesting to look at, but it functions well.

SOME CONCEPTS TOOK ADVANTAGE OF THE STRUCTURAL PROPERTIES OF THE CARDBOARD BOX.

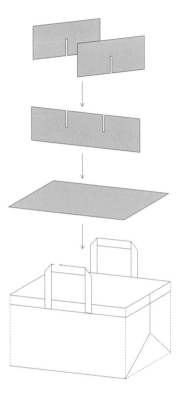

READY-MADE PROTOTYPE. We tested a box with dividers and integrated handles designed by IKEA for packing fragile glassware. This idea worked well for fruits and veggies.

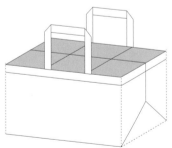

FREE BOXES left over from shipping are offered at many stores. At almost no additional cost, these boxes could be preprinted with patterns and D.I.Y. instructions for repurposing them into useful objects. We combined a large multipurpose shopping bag with parts of a cardboard box to give the bag stability and create dividers. The box can be used to hold things in the car or for general storage. Design: Marleen Kuijf and Kimberly Ruppert, MICA.

Concept: Repurposed Box

PROS. A cardboard box folds flat. It's reusable, it has recycled content, and it's recyclable. The box is structural, so it can be stacked in the store, car, and at home. It's easy to include dividers for objects inside. Printing instructions for a D.I.Y. project on it could add more value. Rethinking packaging as a valuable material as well as an educational object is a big plus.

CONS. A box is not easier to carry than a bag. A box is more expensive to produce than a plastic bag, and it weighs more. It can fall apart if it gets wet.

POSSIBLE SOLUTION. Redesign the farm produce box to have flexible features. Make the box useful for users to repurpose. Graphics or perforations to create handles could add value to the box.

Many stores and consumers have embraced the idea of bringing reusable shopping bags to the store. Can these bags have additional uses when they are brought home? We developed several ideas for hybrid and multifunctional bags. We listed pros and cons for each idea.

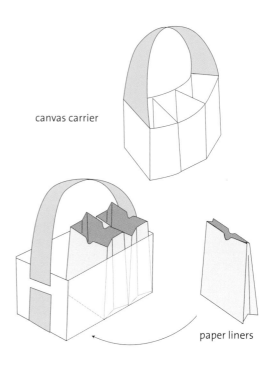

canvas carrier

paper liners

TESTING. We learned a lot just carrying weighted bags around our studio. If an average shopping trip yields four–five bags of groceries, distribution of weight is a challenge. By changing the construction of the canvas bag, we were able to carry four fully loaded paper bags comfortably. But ideally the bag should work with carrying just one paper bag as well as carrying four. Design: Zeynep Akay and Shin Hei Kang, MICA.

Concept: Hybrid Canvas/Paper Bag

PROS. A minimal paper bag without printing and handles (no chemicals used) can be safely composted.

CONS. Hard to carry.

POSSIBLE SOLUTION. Produce an adjustable, reusable canvas box/bag for securing and carrying disposable bags. Design compartments around the human body for optimum weight distribution.

REUSABLE BAGS CAN BE EQUIPPED WITH DIVERSE FUNCTIONS, BECOMING COMPELLING SCULPTURAL OBJECTS IN THEIR OWN RIGHT.

FISH BAG. Like a big fish, this backpack has an open mouth at the shoulder that lets users slide food items into it while shopping. The pack unzips for unloading at home. Design: Sunny Chong, Geoff Kfoury, and Stephanie Sevich, MICA.

Concept: Top Loader

PROS. Easy loading of produce from the top makes it fun to use this bag. Different compartments, including an insulated front pouch, make the bag versatile.

CONS. User needs to be careful when loading produce; firm and heavy items need to go in first.

POSSIBLE SOLUTIONS. Create a truly functional bag for many trips to the store or farmers' market. Perhaps it needs to be made from a single material for easy washing.

BASE STRUCTURE. Our structure needed a bottom, so we looked into creating a cardboard carrier with a paper insert for holding and protecting produce.

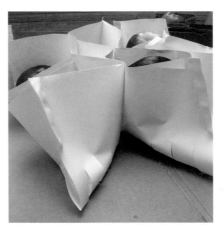

2D TO 3D. One way to wrap paper around a tomato is to make slits to allow the paper to expand.

SLITS were not the best idea because they make paper weak and they make canvas fray. Gussets can work with many materials. We used paper for figuring out the pattern.

MATERIALS. We experimented with open-weave cloth for breathability.

TIP: For your mock-ups, use any material or technique that will allow you to try many ideas quickly. Our favorites are glue guns and duct tape, sewing and stapling.

THIS CANVAS BAG HAS BUILT-IN COMPARTMENTS FOR PRODUCE. IT TURNS SHOPPING INTO A CAREFUL AND PRECIOUS EXPERIENCE. THE BAG ALSO CAN BE USED TO DISPLAY AND STORE PRODUCE AT HOME.

TESTING IN THE STORE. The bag should work as a shopping basket as well as with a cart, too. We filled the bag with bottles and jars as well as with produce, and it worked for both. However, it would work better if some compartments were adjustable. It was fun to gather produce and put it in our bag, but it was also time-consuming and limited how much we could buy. (But maybe buying less is okay.) Design: C. J. Love, Haiji Park, and Hilary Siber. MICA.

Concept: Specialized Canvas Bag

PROS. The bag looks beautiful filled with fruit and vegetables. It is reusable and multipurpose. Despite our worries, the cashier was able to scan most items directly from the bag. Also, the bag fits perfectly in a new double-decker shopping cart.

CONS. Using the bag in the store takes time. The bag is complex to produce.

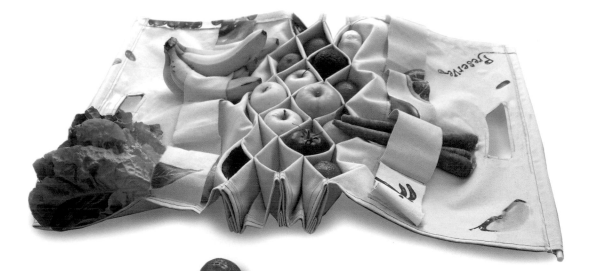

MAKING IT. Sewing the canvas prototype took some skill. Collaborate with model makers, sample makers, and other designers to achieve your goals. Work in a team!

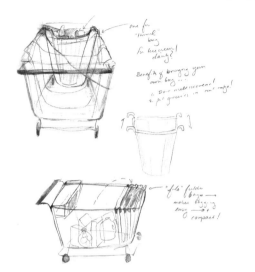

OPEN BAGS. During our visit to the supermarket, we saw that one problem with bringing our own bags is that it slows down the cashier at the checkout. If the bags were already propped open in the cart, checkout might be faster.

FILING SYSTEM. This system is like filing your groceries. The colors could help shoppers remember what they need. Will this system work with every shopping cart? It works with this one.

REAR VIEW. We tested our bag in the supermarket. The bag needed to be comfortable to carry. Carabiner hardware (D-rings) allows the user to attach multiple bags to one superstrap.

EASY TO CARRY. When it's time to leave the store, one strap feels too heavy. Maybe we need more straps to distribute the weight better. The latching system allows for this. Design: Kallie Sternburgh, MICA. Photo: Dan Meyers.

THIS CONCEPT WAS INSPIRED BY A HANGING FILE FOLDER SYSTEM.

Concept: Multibag System

PROS. This multiuse bag is attractive and functional. It works well for shopping with a cart in the store and for carrying groceries home.

CONS. Too many straps and carabiners could be a hassle.

STRAP CONNECTION. We could not find grommets large enough to test our superstrap concept, where more than one carabiner fits into one eyelet.

RETHINKING THE TOILET. The Peepoo bag is a low-tech system developed for communities without septic systems. It converts human waste into a valuable resource. The inside of this single-use, self-sanitizing, biodegradable bag is coated with urea, a non-hazardous chemical commonly used as fertilizer. Urea neutralizes the pathogens in human waste. When the bags degrade in the soil, the contents become a harmless fertilizer. The bag is made from a bioplastic that breaks down into carbon dioxide, water, and biomass. Peepoo could stimulate informal economic systems engaged with collecting used bags for fertilizer. Photo: Peepoople/Camilla Wirseen.

KNOW YOUR VALUES

WHY DESIGN?

What motivates people to become designers? Most designers enjoy sketching, making, inventing, and collaborating. They also want to have a positive impact on the world and are thus concerned about how a project contributes to society and the health of the planet. Let's say you are designing children's furniture. You would think about the following values as you develop ideas:

SUSTAINABILITY. You want to use resources wisely and account for your product's long-term ecological impact. You research clean materials that can be recycled or that can decompose, or materials that are available locally.

EDUCATION. You want kids to learn with your furniture. (Perhaps they will put it together themselves or build things with it.) You look for safe, resilient, colorful materials that appeal to children.

MULTIFUNCTIONALITY AND SIMPLICITY. Your product will grow with kids so it doesn't become obsolete. Or, your product is timeless and simple, so it continues to be functional as its users change.

ACCESSIBILITY. Your product will work for most kids, including those who are physically challenged.

SOCIAL RESPONSIBILITY. The workers who make your product will earn fair wages. The product will be affordable for many people, and you will use materials that are inexpensive.

A designer's wish list for improving the human and ecological condition really has no end. The design process is full of compromises, forcing designers to weigh options against each other. For example, an object that is very durable can perhaps be passed on to the next generation. The design has to be simple so that it will not become outdated quickly. Yet, an object made from renewable resources can create income for a developing community. It could be composted when it is no longer useful. This chapter looks at some of these values in the context of design challenges.

SUSTAINABILITY

Designing for sustainability has become a primary value for many designers, consumers, and manufacturers. Evaluating sustainability means looking at how a product will affect ecological, social, and economic systems in the future. Also known as green or eco-design, sustainable design avoids the consumption of nonrenewable resources, minimizes the release of carbon and other pollutants into the environment, and fosters connections between people and the living world. Studying the life cycle and energy use of a product—from the extraction of materials to the disposal of objects that are no longer needed—are ways to determine whether it is sustainable.

GDIAPERS address the problem of sustainable diaper design by combining a washable, breathable outer pant with a flushable, plastic-free diaper refill. The refill is made from sustainably farmed wood fluff pulp, cellulose rayon, and sodium polyacrylate for absorbency. Where flushing is not available, the wet diaper can be composted in a home garden. gDiapers are cradle-to-cradle certified, meaning that everything that goes into making the refill component can be reabsorbed by the planet in a neutral or beneficial way. Photo courtesy of gDiapers..

DESIGN CHALLENGE

Identify products that require excessive energy for transport, manufacture, disposal, or materials extraction.

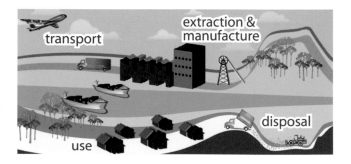

USE A LIFE CYCLE ASSESSMENT (LCA) calculator to compare products. Transportation could account for most of the energy use for products shipped from overseas, while recycling can consume more energy than disposal. Which product will be more sustainable: a bamboo bowl made by craftsmen in Vietnam for export or a bowl made locally of recycled plastic?

REDUCE THE CARBON FOOTPRINT of each product. Green design is not all about making goods out of bamboo and hemp. Materials alone do not assure sustainability, which also encompasses efficient distribution, manufacturing, and other systems.

THE LCA CALCULATOR allows users to assess a product's environmental impact by calculating its energy input and carbon output from across its life span (www.lcacalculator.com). It was created by Industrial Design Consultancy, a firm specializing in sustainable design and life cycle assessment. Various other companies and organizations have created similar tools for calculating carbon footprints.

A CARBON FOOTPRINT MEASURES THE ENVIRONMENTAL IMPACT OF A PRODUCT OR ACTIVITY IN TERMS OF THE CARBON DIOXIDE PRODUCED DURING ITS LIFE CYCLE. CARBON FOOTPRINTS HELP INDIVIDUALS AND ORGANIZATIONS UNDERSTAND HOW THEIR CHOICES AFFECT CLIMATE CHANGE.

LESS WASTE. Concentrated soap is marketed as a green product because it reduces freight costs and thus produces lower carbon emissions. Consumers, however, often use just as much concentrated soap as they would use conventional soap—thus wasting material and releasing more pollutants into the environment.

Designer Xanthe Matychak's Clean Dish Soap project proposes a different visual and tactile language to encourage sustainable behavior.

A user mixes the concentrate with water at home (tablet and tap water), creating a normal-strength product. The act of mixing emphasizes the product's value.

The bottle is made from heavy, sandblasted glass. This feels different in the hand than conventionally used HDPE plastic. Perhaps it is less likely to be thrown away quickly.

The spout is designed to dispense soap slowly, encouraging restraint.

The packaging on the soap packet is made from small-diameter craft paper (young trees cut to maintain a healthy forest) and does not use glue (which would be difficult to remove for recycling).

The message on the bottle reads, "You don't need more bottles, you just need more soap."

SEVEN STEPS IN THE LIFE CYCLE OF A GREEN PRODUCT from The Okala Design Guide, www.idsa.org/whatsnew /sections/ecosection/okala.html:

1. Innovation
2. The Right Materials
3. Clean and Green Production
4. Efficient Distribution
5. Low-Impact Use
6. Made to Last
7. Avoiding the Landfill

SHIPPING WEIGHT contributes to a product's carbon footprint. Conventional soap (70% water) is compared here with Clean Dish Soap, a concentrate that is diluted at home in a reusable bottle.

DO IT YOURSELF. User adds tablet concentrate to water at home. Design: Xanthe Matychak. Photo: Esther McMullen/ETC Photo@RIT.

SLOW GOING. The spout inhibits waste by dispensing a small amount of material. This design thus focuses on the product's "use phase," while most concentrated soaps focus on diminishing packaging and shipping costs.

BIOMIMICRY

Many successful products borrow their shape and function from nature. Velcro was conceived when burrs from a plant stuck to an inventor's clothing. "Living machines" are a form of wastewater treatment that imitates the natural cleansing functions of wetlands. Why should designers want to become biologists? The answer is simple: we need to learn from the pros. And who is the best designer of all time? Nature, of course! For more information and ideas, visit BiomimicryInstitute.org.

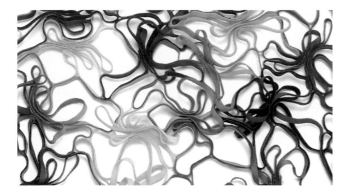

VELCRO OBJECTS by Rachel O'Neill (Loopla collection) assemble like living things.

CORRUGATIONS in nature (top) and in everyday objects (bottom) are smart examples of structures that would otherwise require more material for support.

DESIGN CHALLENGE

Evolution is a design process. Imagine that you are Mother Nature designing a "package" for a worm. What would be the most economical and structural solution? Choose a natural object, such as a snail shell, and analyze not its shape but the problem nature solved when creating it.

Think about flaws in the design and possible solutions that preceded today's adaptations. What human-made materials and structures use similar principles? Make an object that uses these principles to solve a human problem.

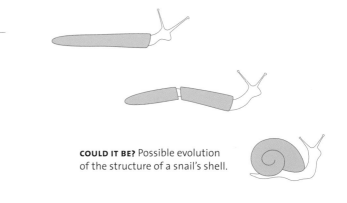

COULD IT BE? Possible evolution of the structure of a snail's shell.

BIOMIMICRY TAKES MANY SHAPES. SOME DESIGNERS APPROACH IT LITERALLY BY INCORPORATING LIVING PLANTS AND ORGANISMS INTO PRODUCTS AND SYSTEMS. OTHERS EMPLOY METAPHOR AND STRUCTURE.

SENSORY LAMP. Sensory stimulation can enhance human creativity and productivity. This task light changes its light quality throughout the day. Grass growing around the mouse pad adds to the experience. Design: Sara Rossbach, MICA.

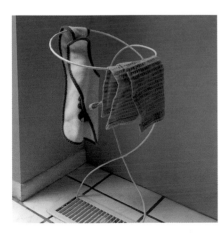

SYMBIOSIS. This drying rack works in concert with a central AC and heating system. Air from the vent can dry small items like a baby bib. The system works like a humidifier. Design: Inna Alesina.

HERBS AND FISH. Some fish can be used for home herb gardens. When the fish eat dead herb roots, their droppings fertilize the water, keeping herbs fresh right in the kitchen. Design: Andrea Dombrowski, MICA.

COLLECT AND PURIFY. What if an umbrella could collect and purify water? This prototype was designed to test if special shapes could be added to a flower pot to collect rainwater. Design: Inna Alesina.

EDUCATION

There are an overwhelming number of toys and games available on the market, and very few of them are educational. Many products bombard kids with images from mass media rather than inspire them to be creative and invent their own worlds. Should designers try to incorporate educational value in all products for kids? Imagine how children will use your product, and invite them into the design process. Talk to parents and kids, and observe children at play.

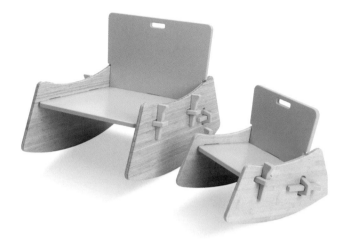

EASY ASSEMBLY. Kids can assemble this children's furniture without using tools. Design: Celery Design.

DESIGN CHALLENGE

Think about areas of learning (math, problem-solving, language skills, music, art, health) and activities of daily life (dressing, grooming, eating, playing, riding in the car, sharing, cleaning up, being safe). Create an object that encourages creativity and growth in two of these areas.

IS IT UNIVERSAL? Will it work for kids of all ages? Will it work for kids of different cultural backgrounds, religions, and languages, of different gender, and with different physical abilities?

IS IT SAFE? Have you avoided toxic materials, sharp edges, and small pieces?

IS IT ADAPTABLE? Will it grow with the child? What about parents? Will it be easy to store and put away?

FRACTION PIE. These cushions are shaped to teach kids fractions through play. Design: Andrea Dombrowski, Kallie Sternburgh, and Madeline Peters, MICA.

TO DEVELOP THIS MULTIUSE ENVIRONMENTAL TOY, THE DESIGNERS OBSERVED KIDS, INTERVIEWED PARENTS, AND CONSULTED PROFESSIONALS FROM A LOCAL CHILDREN'S MUSEUM.

LABYRINTH PICNIC TABLE consists of several dozen foam blocks that are inserted into pockets to create one continuous surface. One minute it is a picnic table for kids (adults can also use it comfortably). When it is no longer needed as a table, kids can easily transform it into a slide, house, or other shape. The toy is fun and safe.

A SIMPLE MAZE can be constructed from Labyrinth by kids or parents. Wooden pegs are included with the product to make more permanent structures. The waterproof fabric can be used as a surface to draw on with chalk. Design: Irina Dukhnevich and Simona Uzaite, MICA.

MULTIFUNCTIONALITY AND SIMPLICITY

Some multifunctional objects are brilliant combinations of form and utility, while others are compromised in at least one of their uses. A pencil with a built-in eraser is more than the sum of its parts, while a sofa bed is good for saving space, but not so good for sleeping. A spork is a poor spoon and a bad fork. Designers look at the continuum of use to decide whether a product works better with one or multiple functions.

WARM FRIDGE. Refrigerators emit a lot of heat, primarily off the back of the unit. This heat is wasted in most environments. In the refrigerator shown here, the tubes are used to warm a seat, converting surplus energy into potential comfort. Design: Michou-Nanon de Bruijn, Design Academy Eindhoven. Photo: Rene Van Der Hulst.

BRILLIANT. Having a pencil with a built-in eraser is like having a low-tech undo button.

DESIGN CHALLENGE

Create sketches or prototypes of objects with more than one function.

COMBINING FUNCTIONS. Example: a plastic bag holder and dog leash.

TRANSFORMING FUNCTIONS. Objects can change throughout the day. Examples: carpet/chair, toy storage/play object, or an object that collapses when not in use.

CHANGING OVER TIME. An object can grow with kids, becoming something else. The Niimi towel designed by Takuya Niimi and Yuki Niimi for Muji is designed for downsizing, changing from a bath towel to a bath mat, and then to a floor cloth and dust cloth.

IMPROVING WITH USE. The "Do Break" vase by Frank Tjepkema and Peter Van der Jagt for Droog Design is made from eggshell porcelain and silicone; when cracked, the ceramic pieces still stay in the shape of the vase because they are held together by the silicone layer.

USING ENERGY generated by the object for other functions. Example: the Warm Fridge shown above.

INTEGRATING INFORMATION into a product. Example: rain poncho with city map printed upside down on the front for easy reference.

LEFTOVERS. What if you used your scrub brush as a soap dish? When the soap is almost gone, it can be used with the brush.

HERE, DESIGNERS CREATED PROTOTYPES FOR OBJECTS WITH MULTIPLE FUNCTIONS.
A SHOWER CURTAIN WARMS A TOWEL. A ROOM DIVIDER BECOMES A CLIMBING WALL
AND STORAGE DEVICE.

KANGAROO SHOWER CURTAIN. Warming a bath towel on a radiator is a common practice, but what if you have a different kind of heating system? What if your towel could be warmed with the shower water? This curtain uses the conductivity of foil to warm the towel inside a waterproof pocket. The design also lets the user access the towel from behind the curtain, thus keeping the user warm when reaching for the towel. Design: Benjamin Howard, MICA.

CLIMBING WALL for kids and adults contrasts with the wall behind it. The panels can be flipped to create an easy or more challenging course. When not in use as sports equipment, it can store clothes, pictures, and other objects. Design: Lily Worledge, MICA.

ACCESSIBILITY

Universal design aims to be good for everyone, regardless of his or her physical abilities. Door bars that function by leaning on them are as useful to a person carrying groceries with both hands as to someone with a physical disability. Cuts in the curb aid people with strollers, carts, dollies, and scooters as well as people in wheelchairs. A lamp that switches on by touching is easier for most people to use than one that requires manipulating a tiny knob. Disabled people are not a separate population. Most individuals will face physical challenges at some stage of life, whether permanent or temporary.

REDUCED STIGMA. While some objects are designed with specific users in mind, making them look and feel attractive helps create a universally designed object. This walking aid looks like sports equipment. It not only supports the body but transports objects.

DESIGN CHALLENGE

Create a product to be used by different people, including a child, an older person, someone in a wheelchair, and a visually impaired person. Observe people doing everyday activities to discover problems that need to be solved.

WIDER CHAIR. This seating system accommodates people of different sizes. Perhaps airplanes, restaurants, and schools should have chairs in multiple widths.

UNIVERSAL PLUG has an opening that enables users to pull it out easily, even with weak hands. A larger opening in the handle would make this plug accessible to even more users. Design: Kim Seung Woo; Red Dot Award for design concept, 2008.

TO CREATE THE PROTOTYPES AND PRODUCTS SHOWN HERE, DESIGNERS IDENTIFIED PROBLEMS AND INTERVIEWED CAREGIVERS AT NURSING HOMES AND HOSPITALS. CONCEPTS WERE CREATED IN AREAS SUCH AS CLEANING, COOKING, SHOPPING, TRAVELING, AND WORKING.

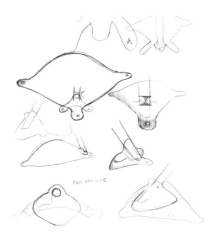  

SPONGE-ANGLE is a mop with a foot pocket. Experimenting with mops, we found that it is easier to apply pressure with one's foot than to push against the stick handle.

The curved handle of an early prototype provided extra space for the foot. This product helps people who have difficulty bending down or applying pressure with

their hands. The product is easier to use for most other users as well. Design: Kallie Sternburgh and Inna Alesina, MICA.

 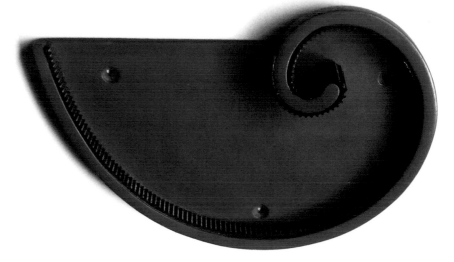

GRIPS are a big problem for people with weak hands. The Nautilus jar opener allows a person to open a jar with one hand. Rubber grips hold the lid in place. The nature-inspired shape was also inspired by the movement of sliding and twisting the jar open. Design: Inna Alesina.

SOCIAL RESPONSIBILITY

Designers solve problems. Many designers want to be involved in meaningful projects that have a positive social impact. However, making special products that we think will benefit the poorest members of society can be difficult for designers who live in a house with electricity, water, and a supermarket nearby. Many useful low-cost designs are made by people living in the developing world.

Designing responsible products doesn't exclude creating elegant objects for wealthy clients. Companies including Artecnica have engaged designers to create high-end products to be crafted by artisans whose skills would otherwise disappear. Other designers and companies create products to be paid for by governments and distributed to needy communities. Yet others create open source proposals that empower local people to become makers and designers, producing their own products from local resources.

Few problems can be solved with design alone. When conceiving a product for any audience, we should think of its social impact. Will the workers who make it get fair wages? Will health and child labor laws be observed in its production?

YELLOW NEEDLE CAP attaches to any soda can, creating an instant sharps container. Used for collecting hypodermic needles, the device prevents needle-stick injuries and the transmission of blood-borne diseases. Design and photo: Hân Pham. INDEX Award winner, 2007.

DESIGN CHALLENGE

Shelter is a basic human need. Natural disasters and poverty create homelessness in both developed and developing regions. Devise temporary portable housing elements for homeless people in your area. Find out where and how these people live by observing and talking with them.

The issue is larger than providing people with blankets and adding contraptions to shopping carts. The problem encompasses social services, education, mental health, and drug use. Working in the isolation of the design studio is not enough. Talking with people who sleep on the streets is an eye-opening experience.

PORTABLE LIVING. Designers at Savannah College of Art and Design worked with the Growing Hope Artisans Cooperative to explore design issues facing homeless people. They looked at the need for portability and safety as well as relationships between permanent and transitional housing. Design: Joemy Buschur, Olivia Cuenca, Andrea Gray, Anna Greer, Chuck Heydinger, Cory Imig, Beth Kane, Rubi McGrory, Alice Meiss, Eric Payne, Ashley Wedekind, Melanie Wilcox, Erin Wiser, and Kay Wolfersperger.

HOMELESSNESS IS AN ISSUE THAT MANY PEOPLE DO NOT WANT TO SEE OR NOTICE, BUT IT IS RIGHT IN OUR OWN BACKYARDS AND NEIGHBORHOODS. THIS PROJECT COMMUNICATES THE IMPORTANCE OF THE ISSUE WHILE PROVIDING A TEMPORARY SOLUTION THAT SHOWS RESPECT FOR THE PEOPLE INVOLVED.

TYVEK EMERGENCY SLEEPING BAG. This prototype was initiated as an entry to a homeless-shelter competition. An informational poster in the shape of a house would be posted throughout urban areas. A person in need of an emergency sleeping bag could peel the poster from the wall. The poster is covered with inspirational stories and practical advice about living on the street. It uses several features of Tyvek: durability, pliability, printability, and water-resistance. Design: Sara Rossbach, MICA.

THINK WITH MATERIALS

EVERYDAY USES AND INSPIRING EXPERIMENTS

What are materials? Every product we use is made from one or more substances, nearly all of which have been processed from their original states in the animal, vegetable, and mineral worlds. Cutting, milling, heating, bending, extruding, and mixing are all techniques for processing (and thus changing) materials. Plastics and composites are made by chemically transforming and physically binding diverse substances to make new ones with new properties. Some products, such as a computer or a car, consist of hundreds of different materials, while others, such as a cardboard box or a leather shoe, consist of only a few. The greater the number of materials a product contains, the more difficult it is to reclaim them for future uses.

The way materials are processed affects their structural properties and behavior as well as their appearance and texture. For example, corrugated cardboard is stronger and lighter than noncorrugated cardboard, even though the chemical composition of the materials is similar. The principle of corrugation (a ridged plane) appears in natural things such as the leaf of a banana plant as well as in other human-made materials such as metal and plastic.

A material is thus not simply a substance having particular chemical characteristics. A material has structure, and designers manipulate that structure to create objects that are functional, economical, and beautiful. Shown on the following pages are materials commonly used in the design of products. We have explored each one in terms of familiar everyday objects whose functionality has been proven over time. Also shown are experimental uses of materials by contemporary designers and ideas for making your own prototypes using readily available tools and accessible techniques. The goal of this book is to inspire designers to think about how materials behave and to use those properties to stimulate the birth of new ideas. Smart, simple concepts are embodied in thousands of objects we use everyday, from paper-pulp egg cartons to clay flowerpots. We challenge you to unlock the genius of ordinary things and common materials and discover new ways to think and create.

CARDBOARD, CORRUGATED

Corrugated cardboard is used for making objects of every scale, from single-use java jackets to full-size buildings. This great invention is most commonly built like a sandwich with waves or fluting lying between two pieces of smooth board. The structural properties of corrugated cardboard vary depending on the direction of the flutes and the number of walls. Corrugated board can be specified according to its construction (single face, single wall, double wall, etc.), flute size, recycled content, and so on.

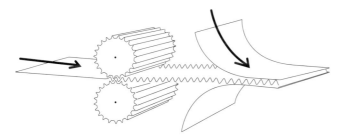

INTERIOR DOORS are commonly made with a corrugated cardboard spacer sandwiched between layers of wood veneer. This makes the door both lightweight and inexpensive.

SINGLE-FACED CARDBOARD is a flexible material used for wrapping objects.

ZAGO TRASH CAN is made from a sheet of single-wall corrugated board with three folds and a tab. Design: Giovanni Pellone and Bridget Means for Benza.

CARDBOARD CHAIR designed by Frank Gehry. Each layer is cut to expose the flutes. Adding layer to layer creates a strong structure and a beautiful surface. Image courtesy of Gehry Partners.

CARDBOARD BECOMES STRONGER WHEN FOLDED INTO VOLUMES.

FOLDED STRUCTURES. This children's furniture is made from folding corrugated cardboard like origami. Free instructions and patterns are available from www.foldschool.com. Design: Nicola Enrico Stäubli.

PROTOTYPE FOR LOCKING MECHANISM. When two open-faced corrugated boards are positioned facing each other, they can lock and slide in one direction. Designers used this method to model a functioning screw fastener in a concept design for a screw-top coffee lid. Design: Alexa Sahadi and Ragnhild Haugum, Parsons School of Design.

PASTE WAX can be brushed on cardboard to make it waterproof. To apply paraffin, heat the cardboard with a heat gun so that the paraffin can soak in. Be careful—cardboard is highly flammable. Soaking the material in linseed oil for several hours also makes cardboard waterproof and gives it a leather like sheen. (This can weaken the glue, so this technique works better for paperboard.)

SHIPPING BOX easily transforms from 2D to 3D. The box is printed with illustrated instructions—user-friendly!

POLYGON CHAIR is made from facets of folded cardboard. Design: Haiji Park, MICA.

CARDBOARD STOOL uses a single sheet of cardboard with no glue or extra fasteners. Design: Kate Sheffield. Photo: Francis Luu. Faculty: Karen Cheng, University of Washington.

DESIGNERS CREATE INTERESTING SURFACES WITH THE EXPOSED EDGES OF THE MATERIAL.

FLUTE PENDANT LIGHT. A baroque-style pattern has been "fluted" into the surface by alternating the angle of the corrugation through the shade. Design: Giles Miller.

PROTOTYPING TECHNIQUES

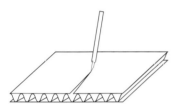

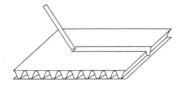

SCORING. Use an X-Acto knife or a blunt object to create a score line in the cardboard and make a clean, controlled fold.

FLUTING. A sheet of cardboard was sliced on a slight angle. Its flutes become visible when it is tilted. Combining pieces with different angles creates a pattern that transmits light differently across its surface.

CARDBOARD SPIRAL. A flat sheet of single-faced cardboard was sliced with an X-Acto knife into one-inch-wide strips. The cut was made perpendicular to the direction of the flutes. The strips were put together to create a honeycomb surface that light can pass through. Design: Inna Alesina.

TIP: Elmer's carpenter glue works well with cardboard. For quick mock-ups, try hot glue. For advice about adhesives see www.thistothat.com.

CARDBOARD, NONCORRUGATED

Noncorrugated cardboard, or paperboard, is strong and biodegradable, easy to work with, and can be salvaged for free. (Save your cereal boxes!) It uses renewable resources, and it can be reused many times. Flat paperboard is made from paper pulp. Paperboard is used for book covers, packaging, and small storage containers, and it can be wound into structural tubes and cones. Graphics can be printed directly on flat board. The surface also can be laminated, perforated, and formed into boxes and tetra shapes.

CARDBOARD CLOTHES HANGERS are recyclable and have a large area for graphics. Until recently, disposable wire hangers were the only choice at the dry cleaners. Design: Hanger Network.

TETRA PAK® is a packaging system made from cardboard laminated with plastic film, suitable for storing liquids. The flat sides of the material can hold a lot of information.

CONES for yarn spools are made from paperboard wound into a cone shape. A tube can be used as a core (toilet paper roll) or protective shell. See more about spiral-wound tubes in the RODS AND TUBES section.

PROTOTYPING TECHNIQUES

LASER ETCHING ON CHIPBOARD. Cardboard can be laser etched or cut with traditional shop tools including a drill, band saw, and dremel. Make sure the cardboard is dry.

LASER-CUT PRESSBOARD CIRCLES were stacked to create this structure. The shapes were made from a computer-generated 3D model. The slices were glued together by hand into a branch like shape to make a base for a side table. Design: Sara Rossbach, MICA.

TIP: Designers collect boxes with interesting features like flaps, perforations, tabs, locks, and automatic bottoms. To understand how to create boxes and other structures from scratch, open boxes along the seam and note how they were made.

School glue, double-stick tape, and staples work well for creating structures with cardboard. For large surfaces, spray mount can be used. Make sure you protect surrounding surfaces, provide good ventilation, and wear a protective respirator. Never spray in a studio full of people. Use a spray booth, or grab old newspapers and step outside.

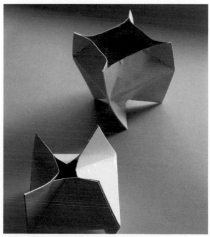

CORNER PROTECTOR is made of multiple layers of paper bonded to form an L shape. Layering also is used to make flat cardboard structurally strong.

MILK CARTON PROTOTYPES. Starting from the existing shape of a milk carton, score the sides to prototype a variety of shapes. Peel away the plastic from the side where you will apply glue to ensure a strong bond.

Velcro, flat magnet strips, clasps, snaps, and zippers can be used to add functionality to cardboard objects. Connnect with glue or rivets, or stitch cardboard by hand or on a sewing machine. Cloth or paper can be used to create a flexible hinge, as in the spine of a book.

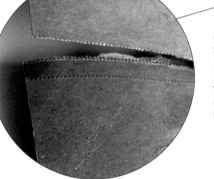

MEDIA MAIL PACKAGE looks like a vacuum-sealed pack. The object inside is hugged between two layers of cardboard. Perforation makes it easy to tear open the package. Depending on the adhesive used, mailing envelopes may or may not be easily recyclable.

BOOK OF MATCHES is held together with a single staple.

RESLEEVE is a "green" CD jacket. It is an alternative to plastic jewel cases. Manufactured by Sustainable Group.

MATH TOY was prototyped with paperboard and then laser cut from fiberboard. Design: Kwok Pan Fung, MICA.

CARDBOARD BOXES HAVE AN ASTONISHING RANGE OF INTERACTIVE FUNCTIONS.

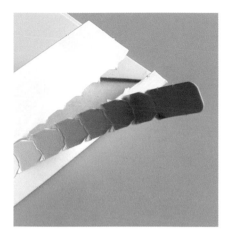

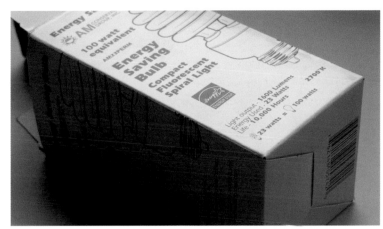

PERFORATION is an intuitive way to make an easy-to-open cardboard package. Sometimes ribbon is inserted under the cardboard to help the user cut through the perforation.

FLAT PACK. A box can be shipped or stored flat and then become a 3D structure. This "automatic" box bottom is designed for fast folding on an assembly line.

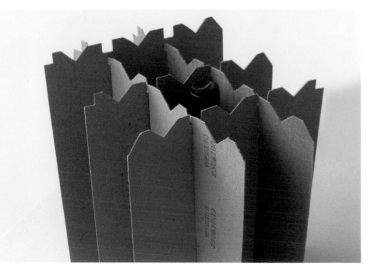

CARDBOARD GASKETS are used in electrical installation. Punched shapes are modified by the user to fit a variety of applications.

SHIP RESPONSIBLY. The next time you pick up a case of wine or a carton of beer, take time to admire the packaging. The pack folds flat, uses very little material to do the job, looks good on the store shelf, and keeps the bottles from breaking during transport.

CERAMICS

The term *ceramics* covers a broad range of materials and techniques in which heat is applied to inorganic nonmetallic materials. This basic principle has been used for thousands of years to form vessels as well as building materials such as bricks and tiles. Glazing transforms the surface qualities of ceramic in ways that are both functional and decorative, making them nonporous and easy to clean.

HIGH-VOLTAGE INSULATORS make use of the nonconductive property of ceramics.

UNGLAZED CERAMICS, such as terracotta, are porous. This is good for potted plants, since the material can help regulate the amount of moisture the plant's roots get.

THE POT-IN-POT SYSTEM is a refrigeration technique invented for use in rural Nigeria. Two clay pots are nested one inside the other; sand and water are placed in the space between them. Water evaporates from the sand and draws heat away from the smaller pot, creating a cool cavity for storing food. Design: Mohammed Bah Abba. Photo: ©Rolex Awards/Tomas Bertelsen.

CERAMICS ARE SHAPED BY HAND AND MACHINE.

IN THE ROUND. In addition to working with their hands, potters have devised tools such as the potter's wheel and the turntable to help make uniformly shaped vessels and other objects.

MODULAR COFFEE MUGS fit together at the handles to create a flowerlike shape. The original prototype was made from styrene. Design: Daniel Harper.

STAMP CUPS have a raised pattern on their bases. Spilled coffee or tea thus makes a charming print as the cups are used. Design: Valeria Miglioli and Barnaby Barford.

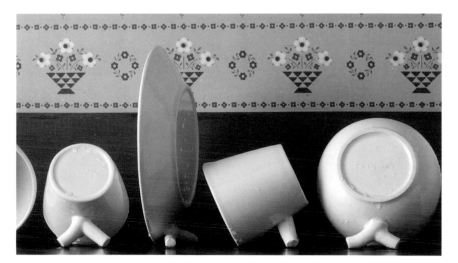

DRIP PLATE, BOWL, AND CUPS. Added functionality is built into these objects, whose handlelike appendages allow them to drain without a rack. Design: Jim Termeer and Jess Giffin.

FLEXIBLE MOLDS were used to make the porcelain objects shown here. Sewn from sponge cloth, the molds change shape during the slip-casting process. All the features of the mold's construction, from the texture of the sponge to folds, creases, and stitching, leave impressions on the cast vessels. Each object is unique. Design and photos: Bas Kools.

Shown here is a mold and the finished, fired mug.

These mugs were all cast at the same time. Because the molds were pressed against each other during the casting process, they influenced each other's shapes.

THE PLASTICITY OF CLAY ALLOWS IT TO TAKE THE SHAPE OF THE HUMAN HAND AND BODY.

TOPOWARE is an experimental prototype for a set of porcelain dishes that address the needs of the visually impaired while eating. Stumbling, fiddling, dropping, and spilling are problems that cause anxiety at the dinner table for people whose vision is impaired. These objects encourage users to slow down and interact with the pieces. No piece has one fixed use. Instead, the user determines the function as he or she becomes familiar with the implement. Lips prevent spills, while walls at the edges of a plate allow food to be pushed against them. The designer worked with paper, plaster, silicone, fiberglass, and porcelain to create dozens of prototypes. A bowl made partially from flexible silicone enables indirect contact with the food. Testing the tools by eating with them was an essential part of the design process. Design: Hilary Siber, MICA.

CONCRETE

Concrete is a widely used construction material that also has applications to objects. The main ingredient of most concrete is portland cement, a material that is mined and processed to achieve its unique properties. When cement mixes with water, a chemical reaction is set in motion that yields a hardened, rocklike material. Concrete can be formulated with other substances such as sand, gravel, fly ash, slag cement, and chemical additives to withstand various conditions, such as high heat, and to create different finishes, strengths, and colors. Concrete can be poured into molds to take any shape. Like stone, it has great compressive strength but limited tensile strength; hence it is often reinforced with steel rebar, especially in building applications. Concrete is attractive for its strength, permanence, weather-resistance, low cost, and plasticity.

LOOP CHAIR. Designed by Willy Guhl in 1954, this chair is made of Eternit, a cement/cellulose composite that is extremely strong and has a smooth, inviting surface. Structurally, it consists of a single band of material. Manufactured in Switzerland by Eternit. Photo courtesy of Eternit.

CUMULUS TABLE was made by pouring concrete into a plastic bag that was held in a plywood jig. The table was created as part of a design challenge to make low-cost objects. Design: Daniel Jeffries, Pratt Institute.

FOAMED CONCRETE contains air bubbles in a cell-like structure, making it five times lighter than ordinary concrete. It can be easily machined into new shapes. Made from an autoclaved cellular concrete block, these stools were turned on a lathe using traditional woodworking tools. Design and photo: Max Lamb.

PROTOTYPING TECHNIQUES

MAKING MULTIPLES WITH SILICONE MOLDS IS A COMMON WAY TO PROTOTYPE OBJECTS FROM EPOXY RESIN, PLASTER, OR CONCRETE.

CONCRETE JEWELRY. Designers Sean Yu and Yiting Cheng of 22designstudio have created concrete rings reinforced with stainless steel. First, stainless steel tubes are placed in the silicone molds.

Next, cement is poured into the mold. The mold is pattered (gently tapped) to make air bubbles rise to the surface. The material is left to set for two days. The concrete is sanded clean and the exposed metal element is polished.

The ring is kept wet for twenty days so that it doesn't dry before it completely cures. Design and photos: Sean Yu and Yiting Cheng, 22designsotudio.

FABRIC, KNIT AND STRETCH

Unlike most woven fabrics, knitted textiles can stretch up to 500%, depending on the material used and the knitting construction. Knits have thus been used traditionally in stockings and other resilient, close-fitting garments. Springy yarns such as Lycra and Spandex increase the stretchiness of knits. Such fabrics are supple and lightweight, yet can be stretched over and over again and still recover their original length. Traditionally used for sportswear, high-performance stretch fabrics are now appearing in home furnishings, car accessories, toys, and other products. Designers are attracted to the material's diverse colors and textures as well as to its ability to create smooth compound surfaces.

RECYCLED FLEECE. Patagonia Synchilla® Marsupial jacket. Patagonia was the first sportswear company to adopt fleece made from post consumer recycled plastic soda bottles. The material was developed in 1993 by Wellman Inc. (Not all fleece is made from recycled material.) Patagonia also accepts some worn polyester clothing for recycling through its Common Threads Garment Recycling Program.

RF WELDED EARWARMER SHELL. These earwarmers are made with removable components that clip to the frame with a rubber groove. Instead of stitching, the stretch shell is RF (radio frequency) welded to the rubber. Design: 180s.

WICKING MOISTURE. New hi-tech polyester cotton blends transport sweat away from the body. Silver threads inhibit the growth of bacteria and make gym clothes smell better.

STRETCH TEXTILES CAN BE EITHER LIGHT AND TRANSPARENT OR DENSE AND OPAQUE.

PERSONAL OFFICE DIVIDER. This canopy provides privacy in an open studio or office. Design: Susannah Munson, MICA.

ROCK PILLOWS. These floor pillows are designed to look like round rocks. They are filled with buckwheat hulls and covered with Schoeller textile, a woven fabric that gets its four-way stretch from Lycra. Design: Inna Alesina. Photo: Gleb Kutepov.

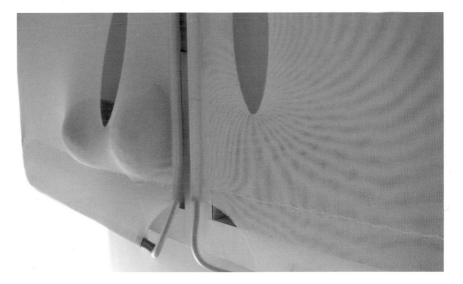

KITCHEN STORAGE. Called Metamorphosis, this kitchen storage system uses a tubular frame and stretch mesh fabric to add storage pockets to existing kitchen cabinets. The breathable mesh allows fruits to be stored longer, while the stretch accommodates a variety of shapes. Design: Inna Alesina and Lauretta Welch.

CHAIRBACK STORAGE. This prototype for a chair caddy was sewn using the chair itself as a guide. Design: Anokhee Desai and Dorota Pisarska, MICA.

TRAVEL PONCHO unfolds to become a blanket and seat support. Nonstretch straps adjust to support people of different sizes. Design: Ewa Wiencis, MICA.

PROTOTYPING TECHNIQUES

Working with knit fabric

Use zigzag or special stretch stitch setting on your sewing machine.

Use thread that is very strong or has some stretch to it.

You can control how fabric will stretch by pulling on it while stitching.

To make your objects look factory-finished, sew stretch binding around the edges. Look at outdoor clothing and see how the collar or cuff on a fleece edge looks. Although bindings can be used on any material, stretch binding is most useful with fleece. A stretch binding is usually made with Lycra and can act as elastic at the same time as finishing the edge.

STRETCH BINDING on a jacket cuff provides an elastic edge.

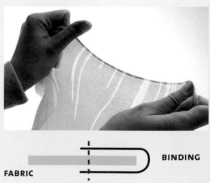

THE RUNS. Knit fabric doesn't fray, but each knitted stitch can run if you pull on the fabric's edge. Finishing the edge helps prevent runs.

STRETCH FABRIC HAS THE ABILITY TO EXPAND AND THEN RETURN TO ITS ORIGINAL LENGTH.

WORK IT OUT. This exercise suit incorporates knitted fabrics into business attire. The black tie becomes a resistance exercise device. The designer created a series of exercises that work on the body parts most affected by prolonged sitting and working on the computer. Design: Larissa Vieira, MICA.

FABRIC, NONWOVEN

Nonwoven textiles are made by gathering many small fibers into a sheet or web and then binding them via heat, glue, or mechanical means. Nonwoven fabrics don't fray when cut, making them appropriate materials for perforating and die-cutting. Like paper or cardboard, they can be embossed or debossed with patterns and textures. Typical uses include feminine and baby products, air filters, and disposable items for the medical industry, where breathable and absorbent material is needed.

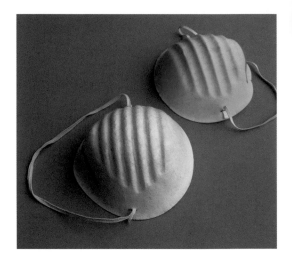

DUST MASK is made from nonwoven material that has been molded into a 3D shape. The corrugation maximizes the filter's surface area and adds structure to the mask.

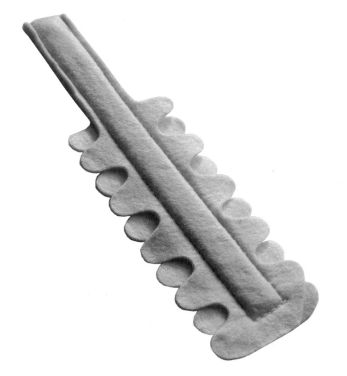

DUST MAGNET. Many cleaning products use nonwoven materials because they create an electrostatic charge that attracts dust, dirt, hair, and common allergens. Many of them are designed to be disposable (Swiffer refills). Shown here is the Mini-Reach duster, which is washable. Design: Unger Industrial, LLC.

RECYCLED PET PLASTIC was used to make the material for this shopping bag. The stitching process makes the nonwoven fabric even more durable.

DESIGNERS USE WELDING, STITCHING, GLUE, AND VELCRO TO CONSTRUCT OBJECTS WITH NONWOVEN FABRIC. SOME OBJECTS ARE MADE SIMPLY BY FOLDING AND CUTTING SHEETS OF NONWOVEN MATERIAL.

DISAPPEARING SURFACE. This fabric is made by embroidering on water-soluble plastic. When the design is completed, the plastic is dissolved in warm water, leaving the embroidered threads as structure. Design: Charlet Richards, MICA.

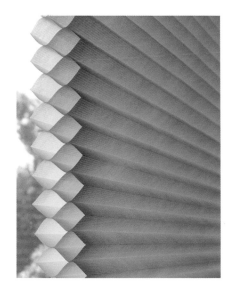

TRANSLUCENT SHADE. This window treatment exploits the translucence of nonwoven fabric. More durable than paper, the material has been welded to create a collapsible honeycomb structure. The cells also provide insulation.

NO MORE COFFEE STAINS. In this prototype, nonwoven fabric has been infused with mint flavor and attached to a paper cap. Users can wipe their teeth with the cloth after drinking coffee. Design: Inna Alesina.

Nonwoven textiles include Tyvek, a brand of flashspun high-density polyethylene fibers. This synthetic material is commonly used as a "house wrap" in building construction as well as for shipping envelopes, wrist bands, car covers, and more. Tyvek is difficult to tear but easy to cut with scissors or a knife. Water vapor can pass through Tyvek, but not liquid water, making it an excellent indoor/outdoor material. Although paper like, Tyvek is also soft and pliable. It can be machine washed and sewn with a conventional home machine. It can be surface printed with color and graphics.

AIR MAIL MIGHTY WALLET™ is made from a single sheet of Tyvek. The designer has published instructions online showing how to make one from an express mail envelope: instructables.com/id/Express-Mail-Envelope-tyvek-Wallet. Design: Terrence Kelleman for Dynomighty.

MIDSUMMER LIGHT SHADE is die-cut from a flat sheet of color-dyed Tyvek. Design: Tord Boontje for Artecnica Inc.

BREATHABLE PRODUCE BAG. This reusable Tyvek produce bag has been perforated to create ventilation. Design: Inna Alesina.

NONWOVEN FABRIC CAN BE CUT AND FOLDED LIKE PAPER—
YET IT IS EXTREMELY DURABLE AND TEAR RESISTANT.

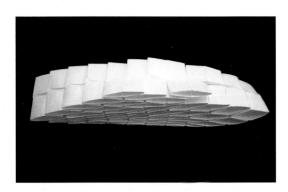

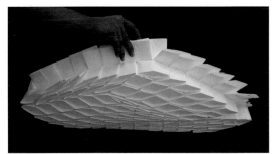

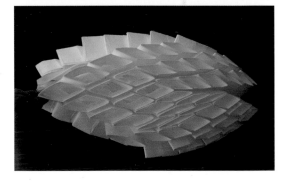

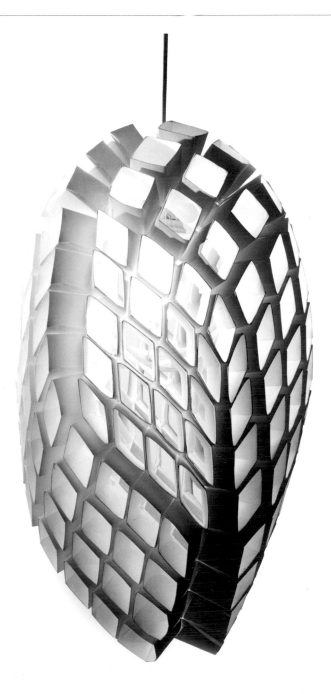

ANEMONE LAMP is made from dozens of four-walled geometric Tyvek shapes connected to create a 3D surface. Inside, a metal sphere serves as the lamp's structural core while keeping the bulb away from the exterior. The lamp can rest on a table or floor or hang from the ceiling. Design: Heath Nash for Artecnica. Photo: Jerry Garns.

FABRIC, WOVEN

Humans have produced woven textiles for thousands of years. Weaving consists of interlaced rows of yarn or thread. Warp threads run along the length of the cloth, while woof or weft threads travel crossways. In addition to its use in clothing, this flat, flexible material is employed in furnishings, accessories, cars, buildings, interiors, and more. There are few industries that do not use textiles in some way.

Designers often combine fabric with other elements. To have structure, fabric has to be either held in tension within a framework (like a sail on a boat) or weighted (like a bag full of books). It can be used as a component in composite materials, where chemicals such as plaster or epoxy make it hard. Composites of fiberglass, Kevlar, and carbon fiber are used to create durable, lightweight vessels such as canoes. Trampolines, folding chairs, and baby strollers use the nonstretch properties of woven cloth to create structural surfaces. Fabric can be made into collapsible tension structures such as tents, folding furniture, and umbrellas.

SAILS. Canvas cloth is used in the construction of this windmill in Cyprus.

FABRIC ARCHITECTURE. To create an architectural structure with cloth, nonstretch fabric is held in tension with poles and cables. Light passes through the cloth, making the space inside comfortable. The cloth structure is stretched over and attached to the metal armature. Waterproof finishes make the structure durable and practical.

SOFT STRUCTURE. A wind catcher has no hard structure except for the ring looped through the fabric channel. Wind gives it structure by temporarily inflating the sleeve.

WOVEN FABRIC IS LIGHT, FLEXIBLE, AND STRONG. IT HAS DIFFERENT BEHAVIORS DEPENDING ON HOW IT IS CUT, SEWN, AND STRETCHED.

TRAMPOLINES use the nonstretch properties of woven cloth. The spring attachments around the rim give the trampoline its bouncy property. If the trampoline surface were stretchy, one would sink into it instead of bounce off it.

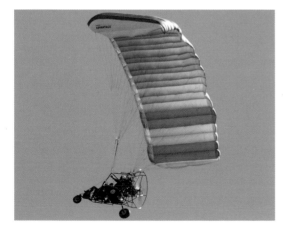

RIPSTOP NYLON is a lightweight nylon fabric with interwoven reinforcement threads whose crosshatch pattern makes the material resist tearing. It is used for sails, kites, parachutes, tents, flags, banners, and other applications that require a strong, rip-resistant fabric.

BIAS. Woven cloth has directional fibers. It usually deforms (stretches) on the bias direction that runs at a 45-degree angle to the selvage (edge). The threads used to make the fabric affect the way the surface folds. When creating objects from cloth, designers pay close attention so that all pieces run on the same bias.

Designers use the behavior of fabric to create objects that respond to the environment. The natural fibers used by nomads for making tents swell during rain, creating a waterproof surface, and shrink when dry, creating a breathable membrane. Cheese cloth is used as a screen to separate curd from whey in the cheese-making process. In India, cotton saris are used to filter water by screening impurities.

FILTER. Cloth filters light as well as liquids. A sun canopy can block up to 90 percent of harmful UV rays. Design: Kelsyus.

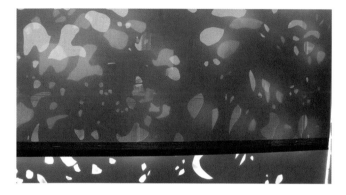

SCREEN. In this prototype for nature-inspired workspace lighting, a gossamer window screen transforms the cutout shapes into an organic canopy. Design: Sarah Rossbach, MICA.

TIGHT WEAVE. Natural fabrics absorb liquids. To waterproof canvas, cover it with several layers of polyurethane on both sides. Some cloth is so tightly woven, it can hold water. This technique is used to create canvas water buckets.

FRIENDLY. This tree house was designed to preserve the tree and leave no footprint. Design: Dre Wapenaar. Photo: Robert R. Roos.

STITCHING, STRAPPING, STUFFING, AND STRETCHING ARE SOME OF THE WAYS DESIGNERS MANIPULATE OBJECTS MADE OF CLOTH.

RAG CHAIR is made of a stack of rags that are bound together with standard strapping tape. Discarded materials are thus reborn into something useful and beautiful. Users can choose to add their own garments to the chair. Design: Tejo Remy for Droog. Photo: Robaard/Theuwkens.

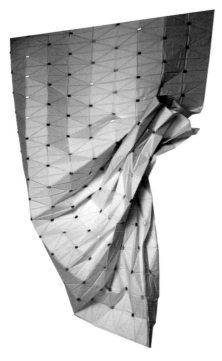

MAGNETIC CURTAIN uses pleats, corrugations, and origami-like folds to give the fabric structure. Magnets allow the user to manipulate its shape. Design: Florian Kräutli for Droog. Photo: Jacek Ryn.

There are countless ways to decorate fabric, from woven patterns to prints, pleats, tie-dye, embroidery, silk screening, stamping, iron-on graphics, and permanent markers. Fabrics with integrated technical functions are materials of the future. Surface imagery can be functional as well as decorative—for example, a tent imprinted with user instructions.

RECYCLED VINYL. This messenger bag is made from repurposed truck tarps. Truck tarp is vinyl-covered cloth that is extremely durable. Each bag is unique. Design: FREITAG.

MINIMAL SHELTER is designed to adapt to the user's surroundings. The structure is supported by a small stick plus stationary objects found in the environment, such as trees, poles, benches, and so forth. Instructions are applied with an iron-on printed label. Design: Lily Worledge, MICA.

SEWING IS THE MOST COMMON WAY TO ASSEMBLE CLOTH. BOTH HAND STITCHING AND MACHINE SEWING ARE PRACTICAL TECHNIQUES FOR THE DESIGNER.

Ways to fasten cloth include mechanical connections such as grommets, staples, and tag guns (used to tag garments in the store), as well as more hi-tech processes like RF (radio frequency) welding. Grommets, rivets, and snaps require special tools, available from craft stores and hardware stores. Shoe repair shops can also install grommets for you.

STITCHING can be done by hand or machine. Techniques including embroidery, quilting, and appliqué add structure as well as decoration to the object. Design: Laura Sansone, House-Wear.

PIPING is a way to make bags and upholstery durable and hold the shape. A flexible rod is covered with cloth and sewn around the edge of the object. Here, the cloth piping has begun to wear out, exposing the plastic core.

ZIPPERS WITHOUT PULLS. Some zippers are used only for assembly. Zippers are often used in car seating to make the fabric fit tightly. It would be difficult to assemble the seats quickly with other methods.

REFLECTIVE. This fabric consists of glass spheres bonded to the surface with a waterproof flexible resin. Such fabrics offer safety to runners, walkers, and bikers at night.

TIP: Elmer's, Sobo, and spray adhesive work best on fabric. For advice about adhesives see www.thistothat.com.

FELT

Felting is an ancient technique invented long before weaving and knitting. Felt is made by placing wool fibers or a blend of wool and other fibers under pressure with steam, causing the fibers to interlock. The felting process can be used to make fabrics in thicknesses up to three inches that can be cut without fraying. Some felt is knitted first and later felted using steam and pressure to make the fibers interlock. A wool sweater can be felted at high heat in the washer and dryer, becoming very tiny but tight and dense, capable of being cut without fraying. Sheets or rolls of industrial felt can be purchased online. Craft felt is commonly available from craft and fabric stores.

Felt is highly absorbent, which is why it is used for industrial gaskets. Specially manufactured round felt, also called felt wicking, is supplied in diameters from one-eighth to one inch. The inventors of "magic markers" discovered how to use absorbent felt fibers as a wick to transport liquid inks onto paper.

DREMEL TOOL for cutting and finishing materials has components made from felt sheets and rolls.

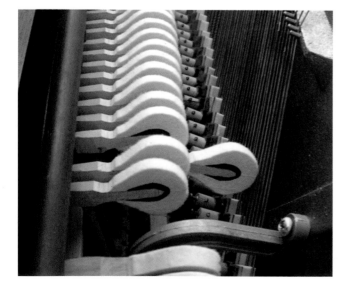

FELT EQUIPMENT. Piano hammers are made from thick sheets of lambswool felt that are shaped and attached to a wooden base. The relative hardness of a piano hammer influences the resulting piano sound.

FELT NECKLACE was die-cut from flat sheets of felt. The design employs small openings and wide circles so that the pieces can be connected in various ways without additional fasteners. Design: Lily Yung. Photo: Swavek Sienkiewicz.

PROTOTYPING TECHNIQUES

INDUSTRIAL FELT COMES IN SHEETS OR ROLLS IN VARIOUS DENSITIES. SHEETS CAN BE DIE-CUT OR SLIT AND CAN BE STITCHED OR LAMINATED.

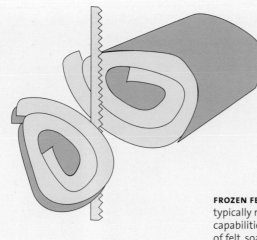

FROZEN FELT. To cut a thick piece of felt typically requires water-jet or die-cutting capabilities. Alternatively, roll up a sheet of felt, soak it in water, and place it in the freezer. When frozen solid, it can be cut with a band saw or even a bread knife.

FELTED BALL was put in the freezer and cut with a bread knife.

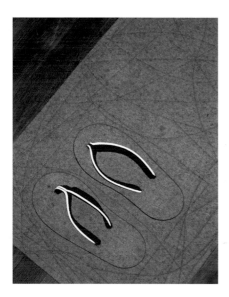

SLIPPER MAT. Designer Laura Sansone integrated flip-flop slippers into a doormat. To make this product, she had the slippers and mat die-cut. Then she sewed on the shoe elements.

SOFT WALL. This flexible wall system consists of an expandable honeycomb paper structure held between sturdy sheets of industrial felt. Design and photo: MOLO.

In addition to being produced in sheets and rolls, felt can be molded into endless shapes. Hand felting has become a popular craft. Traditionally used for producing hats and boots, molded felt can be made into toys, home furnishings, and decorative objects as well as components of musical instruments and polishing tools. Separate woolen pieces can be permanently fused together by felting. Objects can be knitted and then felted later to make them stronger. In the process of hand felting, other objects such as wire can be covered by felt, creating a volume around an inner structure.

UTAN FELTED TOYS are made by hand felting around flexible wire. Design: Yasuyuki Senda.

DELIGHT. This delicate lampshade was made with a traditional wool felt hat base and shape cutters similar to those used in shoe making. Design: Nahoko Koyama, Mixko.

FELT STOOLS are small columns of laminated wool felt discs of varying diameters. The designer machined each disk on a lathe and glued them together using an industrial press. Design and photo: Max Lamb.

THE WARMTH, TACTILITY, AND STRENGTH OF FELT MAKE IT AN APPEALING MATERIAL FOR PRODUCT DESIGN. ITS PRIMEVAL CHARACTER IS ALSO ENTICING.

SLICE FELT CUSHION. Danish designer Lene Frantzen made colorful felted rolls and later sliced them with a water-jet cutter to make colorful seat cushions. Photo courtesy of Danish Craft Council.

FELTED OBJECTS. Felted fibers attach to each other, creating a seamless surface. Any object—such as these ordinary chairs—can be embedded in felt. Designer: Tanya Aguiñiga.

FOAM, CLOSED CELL

Foam is any substance made of bubbles. Foaming agents are added to plastic to create cells. The process is similar to blowing air into a glass of milk. The way the bubbles connect together determines the behavior of the material. In closed cell foam, the bubbles do not touch each other, so air and water cannot pass through the material. Closed cell foam is thus nonabsorbent and nonpermeable. This material is a good insulator because the cells create an air-filled barrier. Its impact resistance makes it useful for packaging and sports helmets. Closed cell foam is hard and holds its shape, yet it is lightweight. Because the cells are nonporous the foam can be used in flotation devices. It is also commonly used as a model-making material. Foam is everywhere, but most of it is not eco-friendly. The manufacturing process creates a permanent crosslink in the polymer, thus yielding a nonrecyclable material.

INSULATION. Foam sheets are widely used in home construction. The cells insulate against heat transfer.

FLOTATION. Pool noodles are made from extruded foam. They have excellent flotation properties and are more durable and reliable than inflatables.

PROTECTION. Soft fruits are often wrapped in molded foam mesh to prevent bruising. Paper tissue is a greener alternative.

INSULATION. The EcoSleeve® is made of a dark-colored Styrofoam that disintegrates into a simple harmless polymer. The dark color makes it less visible on the ground.

DESIGNERS USE CLOSED CELL FOAM FOR INDOOR AND OUTDOOR PRODUCTS. THE MATERIAL IS LIGHT, FLEXIBLE, AND WATER-RESISTANT.

PLOOP. To create this chair, the designer used CAD software to create a two-dimensional outline, which he then sent via email to a fabricator. Working with a CNC foam-cutting machine, the fabricator cut the chair out of closed-cell polyurethane foam glued to form a solid block. This design, which is generated from one continuous cutting line, takes advantage of the foam's elastic properties where the material becomes thin, and its strength where the material is thick. The chair is thus able to bounce back into shape when not in use. Design: Ronen Kadushin. Photo: Baruch Natah.

THE EVERLASTING GOBSTOPPER. Tubes of foam rubber (used for insulation) were woven together by hand to create this soft pouf. Design and photo: Helene Ige.

STYROFOAM ALTERNATIVE. Greensulate is a packaging alternative to conventional foam. This remarkable fungus grows indoors, in the dark, from local biomass products. It can be manufactured without petrochemicals and composted when no longer needed. It can be grown into almost any shape, and it is cost competitive with EPS foam. Shown here is the Greensulate cooler for shipping frozen goods. Design: Eben Bayer. Photo: Ed Browka.

PROTOTYPING TECHNIQUES

BLUE FOAM (or the pink foam that is readily available from hardware warehouse stores) can be cut with a hot wire or hot knife. To refine the shape, use a file and then sandpaper. Sanding in only one direction will make a smoother surface.

PROTOTYPING WITH FOAM. A foam flip-flop is an inexpensive source of closed cell foam. We sliced it on a band saw so that we could use the pieces to create a new shape.

Next, we sanded the pieces on a grinder or sanding machine and then carved a new shape with a dremel tool.

PROTOTYPING TECHNIQUES

FOAM IS OFTEN USED AS A PROTOTYPING MATERIAL, SINCE IT CAN EASILY BE CARVED, CUT, AND SANDED INTO DIFFERENT SHAPES. IT IS CHEAP, LIGHTWEIGHT, AND WIDELY AVAILABLE.

FOAM FORTUNE COOKIE. To prototype this fortune cookie shape, we cut a circle out of a thin sheet of craft foam. We folded it into the desired shape and held it for a minute in hot water. Continuing to hold the shape, we put the foam under cold water. The foam now keeps shape.

DECOUPAGE. To create a new surface, we cut out shapes from Styrofoam deli containers. Foam can be embossed with a serrated knife, hair comb, or piece of metal mesh. Embossed sheets can be cut and glued to other objects to visualize the applied texture.

FLOCKING helps unify a prototype made from patches of different materials. First, apply contact cement on the surface of the prototype. Second, sprinkle it with the foam dust created by the sanding process.

TIP: For prototyping, Liquid Nails contact cement works best with polyurethane and soft foams. Molded objects are often coated with a silicone mold release from the manufacturing process, creating a smooth surface skin. Sand off the skin from the foam before gluing. Wash and dry the foam before applying glue to it.

Make sure you use gloves, respirator, and other means to protect yourself from the fumes and chemicals.

NEOPRENE is a thin layer of foam rubber laminated to a knit fabric for durability and ease of assembly. It is commonly used for wet suits, sports equipment, wine bottle carriers, and laptop cases.

RIVETS are good for connecting foam to foam or foam to other materials. A round hole distributes the tension; other shapes will make the foam rip.

FOAM, OPEN CELL

In open cell foam, the bubbles all touch each other, creating passageways through which water or air can pass. Open cell foams are thus absorbent and permeable. They are also flexible and resilient—you can press down on them and they will bounce back to their previous state. Open cell foams are commonly used in seat cushions and padding. They are usually wrapped or coated in another material, because the foam easily breaks down. Like closed cell foam, most open cell foam materials are synthetic and cannot be recycled.

WELDED FOAM. Sandwiched between two layers of plastic film, a foam sheet is RF welded to make a bladder insert for a sports glove. Working as a spacer, the foam keeps the plastic sheets apart.

VENTILATION. A thin wall of open cell foam allows air to pass through these goggles, preventing moisture from fogging the lens. Design: Oakley.

FOAM PIT provides a soft landing area for kids to play in.

SPONGE CLOTH is made of cellulose. It can absorb and hold liquids, expanding to ten times its size. The material is also biodegradable.

OPEN CELL FOAM OR MEMORY FOAM PROVIDES COMFORT BY CONFORMING TO ANY SHAPE.

COOSH. Inspired by kids' desire to touch, this object is cut from a single block of high-density foam, giving birth to a lounge chair and ottoman or an interlocking curving chaise. The Coosh is a comfortable gamer's chair. Roll it open, lock on the ottoman, and sit back and play. Design: Andrea Valentini.

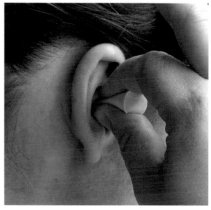

OPEN CELL FOAM is often used to make breathable spacers. Today, most sportswear and shoes use spacer mesh instead of foam to keep the top and bottom material at a distance. Also called air mesh, it is a knit fabric typically made from nylon and polyester.

MEMORY FOAMS are available with many different properties. Some are very slow to recover, and they have a gel-like consistency that makes them heavier than other foams. They are used for hearing protection plugs, pillows, and mattresses.

Open cell foams are used for upholstery, usually covered by fabric. In manufacturing, foams are often laminated with adhesives directly to other materials to add color and a protective surface. Foam can be formed directly in a mold lined with fabric. A complete, fully assembled seat cover is placed in the mold and held in position by a vacuum drawn through small holes in the mold. Polyurethane chemicals are then injected into the mold cavity. Open cell foam is not the best choice for outdoor use because it disintegrates with UV exposure, and moisture can encourage mold growth in it. Used mostly for comfort, soft foam has little structure by itself. It is sometimes molded around another plastic shape or used to cover a harder inner structure.

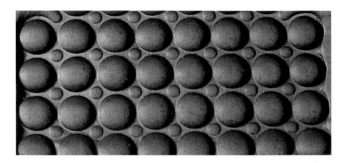

SANDWICH MOLD. The massage bumps on this car seat cover were molded and covered with stretch knit fabric in a one-step process called foam-in-fabric or direct molding. Later, the back surface was covered with a denser foam sheet and sewn or bound around the perimeter to create the finished object.

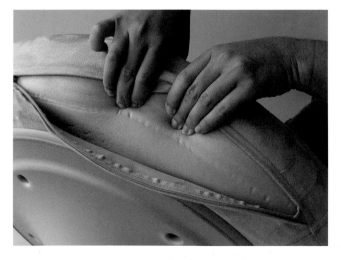

SELF-SKINNING FOAM is an open cell polyurethane foam that creates its own skin in the molding process. The foam bubbles are more condensed where the foam presses against the mold, thus creating a skin. The foam can be molded around plastic parts and is widely used in furniture manufacturing.

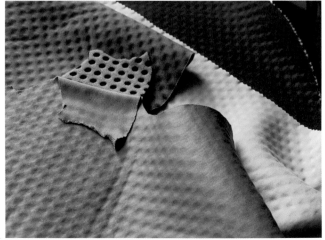

DIMPLED AND BRIGHT. This brilliantly colored sports material was made by laminating stretch knit fabric to both sides of a foam layer. The texture was created by die-cutting circles through the foam.

PROTOTYPING TECHNIQUES

GLUE AND STAPLES ARE COMMON METHODS FOR PROTOTYPING WITH FOAM. DENSER FOAM CAN BE CUT AND SANDED USING POWER TOOLS.

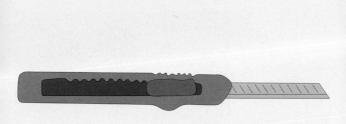

CUT SOFT FOAM with a utility knife with the very sharp blade extended all the way out or a special oscillating foam knife.

TIP: For prototyping products using open cell foam, apply adhesive spray on both surfaces you are attaching. Secure sides with a staple gun. Make sure you use gloves, respirator, and other means to protect yourself from the fumes and chemicals.

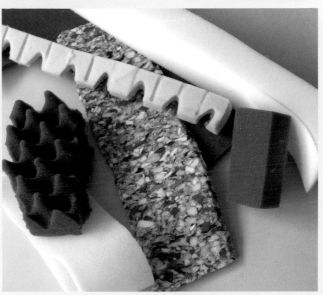

DIFFERENT DENSITIES of foam are good for different applications. Foam cannot be recycled into new foam, but it can be chopped up and glued into down-cycled padding used for carpeting installation.

WRAPPED PROTOTYPE. Large pieces of foam are expensive. It is easy to spray mount separate pieces of foam together to create larger shapes for mock-ups. You can also shrink-wrap loose pieces of foam to create shapes for quick prototypes, making use of scraps of leftover material.

DIP AND SPRAY. These toy fruits were made by dyeing the inside of existing foam balls with fabric dye. When soaked in water, the toy simulates a juicing experience for kids. The skin on the foam makes the toys feel like fruit. The mold for making the balls was sprayed with plastic; the coating bonded with the foam when the foam expanded. Design: Song Hae, Benjamin Howard, MICA.

GLASS

Countless household objects are made of glass, including drinking vessels, bottles, light bulbs, window panes, camera lenses, mirrors, and more. Many of these objects exploit the transparency of glass, which can also be made in translucent or opaque forms. Glass is made by melting sand (silica) with a mixture of soda, potash, and lime. Objects made with transparent glass date back to 800 BCE. Additives such as iron, chromium, and cobalt are added to make brown, green, or blue glass. Glass can be recycled indefinitely because its structure does not deteriorate when reprocessed. Up to 80 percent of the total mixture used in making a bottle or jar can come from reclaimed scrap glass, called "cullet." Making glass from cullet requires less energy than making it from sand.

In manufacturing, glass objects can be blown, cast, pressed, and molded. Blown glass is made by inflating a molten gob of glass like a balloon. Other methods involve pressing molten glass into molds or shaping sheets of glass with heat. In a studio setting, glass can be cut, drilled, sanded, and glued.

FRESNEL LENS. Originally developed for lighthouses, the Fresnel lens is a series of lenses that create a large aperture and short focal length without an extreme weight and volume of material. The Fresnel lens is thinner and lighter than earlier lenses, thus passing more light and allowing lighthouses to be visible over longer distances. It is also used for solar cookers and traffic lights.

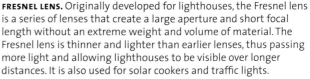

CLUSTER TABLE LIGHT. This light fixture is designed to sit on a table or other flat surface. It is made from multiple handblown globes of glass that are fused together like barnacles during the glass-blowing process. The clear glass bulbs inserted into the piece are an active part of the design. Design: Lindsey Adelman Studio.

PROTOTYPING TECHNIQUES

DRILLING A GLASS OBJECT IS TRICKY EVEN FOR GLASS ARTISTS. WE MADE A LOT OF MISTAKES BEFORE MASTERING THIS TECHNIQUE.

COLD WORKING (drilling and cutting) glass objects does not require expensive equipment. All you need is a cutting tool, a bucket of cold water, and a jig (made of dense foam) to hold object in place. A spear-shaped drill bit is used first for fast drilling, and a diamond-shaped drill bit is then used for slow, second-step "cleaning."

WANT/NEED GLASS has a hole above the line to make the user conscious of the waste created by consuming more than is needed. The glass was silk-screened with the graphics first. To drill a hole in the wall of the glass, we immersed it in water and supported it in the tub with foam blocks. Clamping the glass down minimizes vibration and makes a cleaner hole. Design: Inna Alesina.

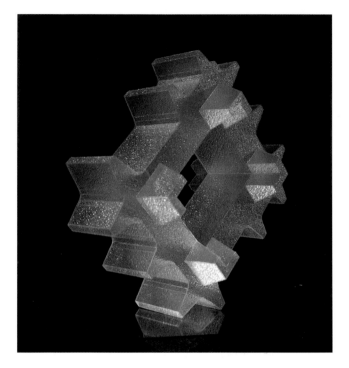

FOUND STYROFOAM ARCHITECTURE. Brenda Goldman works with found materials including Styrofoam packing forms, which she uses as a structure on which to build three-dimensional glass sculptures. She carefully measures iridized clear-textured glass sheets and cuts them by hand to envelop the Styrofoam form like a skin. The entire structure is bonded together with a clear epoxy, which is cured with ultraviolet light, giving the object a seamless appearance much like that of cast glass.

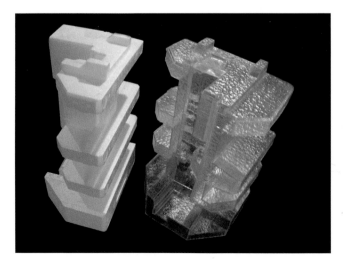

Shown here is the original object and the glass skin that was built around it.

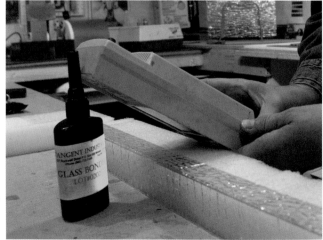

UV-cured epoxy glue is used for precision bonding of glass.

YOU CAN RECYCLE GLASS BY CUTTING AND REPURPOSING PARTS OF EXISTING BOTTLES, CRUSHING OLD GLASS OBJECTS AND FUSING THEM IN A GLASS KILN, OR RECLAIMING THRIFT STORE FINDS.

TILES FROM RECYCLED GLASS. Used beer and wine bottles are collected, cleaned, and broken down, and then fused into beautiful tiles in a glass kiln. Design: Brenda Goldman.

TIP: Glass contains lead; wear a respirator and goggles. Carefully clean up all dust.

UPSIDE-DOWN OBJECTS. Haelan Kim of Studi-oh recycled beer bottles by cutting and polishing them to create small containers. Learn more about cutting at www.instructables.com/id/How-to-use-a -wet-tile-saw-to-cut-glass-bottles.

HONEYCOMB STRUCTURES

Honeycomb structures use a minimal amount of material to create surface materials that are strong and light. Honeycombs appear in nature—most famously in the cellular buildings of honey bees. Similar structures are used extensively in the design of products, from corrugated cardboard and plastic to airplane wings.

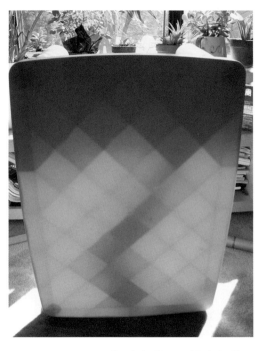

DIAMOND ARMATURE of an injection-molded plastic table is visible against the light. Design: IKEA.

CRAFT PAPER HONEYCOMB is used to create a lightweight structure for shipping fragile objects.

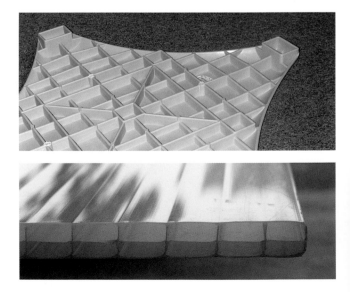

SUPPORT SYSTEM. Reinforcing ribs provide structure to an exercise board (top) and corrugated plastic (bottom).

OBJECTS DESIGNED TO EXPAND AND CONTRACT OFFER FLEXIBILITY IN SMALL LIVING SPACES.

PAPER SOFTSEATING Is made from folded kraft paper. Each piece fans open to create a functional stool, bench, or lounger. The furniture units can be easily folded into compact volumes that are small enough to store on a bookshelf. A similar principle is used in paper party decorations. Design and photo: MOLO.

AR-INGO LIGHT is made from an aluminum honeycomb structure. Design: Ron Arad and Ingo Maurer.

HONEYCOMB PAPER VASE wraps around any ceramic or glass vase.

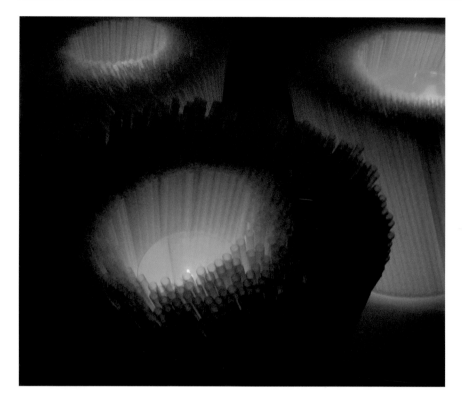

1000 & 1 STRAW LIGHT. Drinking straws packed in a box create a hexagonal matrix. In this experiment, we fused straws together by heating them in a frying pan. The object is made of 1,000 straws and one soda bottle. A compact fluorescent bulb must be used with this material because a hotter lamp will melt it. Electrical wiring and hardware is attached to the soda bottle. Design: Inna Alesina.

WORKING WITH STRAWS. The plastic straws were inserted into a mold made of a frying pan and a steel can, which has the same diameter as a soda can.

After the straws and can were positioned, the pan was heated on the stove. Straws melt where they touch the hot pan.

Applying pressure on the top of the straws created a smooth, thick bottom surface. When the pan cooled, the fused straw structure popped out easily.

PROTOTYPING TECHNIQUES

ONE WAY TO PROTOTYPE A HONEYCOMB STRUCTURE IS TO ATTACH A BUNCH OF ROUND TUBES TOGETHER. AS IN NATURE, AIR BUBBLES WILL FORM INTO A HEXAGONAL MATRIX. STRAWS CREATE A PATTERN IDENTICAL TO A HONEYCOMB.

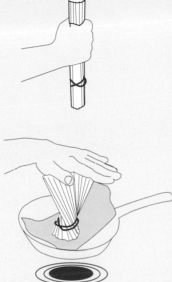

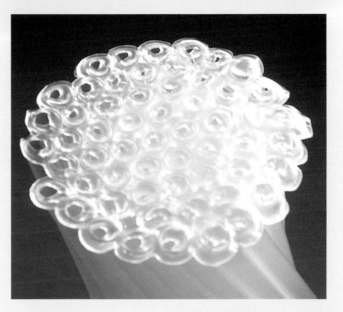

OPEN OR CLOSED? Applying a little pressure on the top of straws when melting them leaves the holes open along the bottom surface. To create a solid bottom, apply more pressure to melt more material.

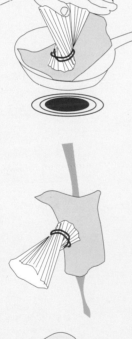

TRY IT. Take a bunch of drinking straws and push one end of the bundle against a hot, foil-lined frying pan. After cooling the fused straws under cold water, peel off the foil.

WASP NEST is a natural honeycomb structure.

INFLATABLE STRUCTURES

An inflatable is an object that can be inflated, usually with air or other gases, such as hydrogen, helium, or nitrogen. Inflatable objects such as balloons, boats, inner tubes, and pool toys take up minimal space when not inflated. Smaller-scale inflatables (such as toys) generally consist of one or more "air chambers" surrounded by a flexible airtight material such as vinyl. Gas can enter or leave the chamber through a valve or other opening. The pressure of the gas makes the inflatable object hold its form. These intriguing structures are thus vulnerable to punctures and tears. Architects and engineers have experimented with large-scale inflatable structures to create temporary shelters and transportation devices. Designers like to exploit the lightness, the ephemeral character, and even the latent humor of inflatable objects.

LARGE BALLOONS filled with heated air or a lightweight gas such as hydrogen or helium have been used as flying machines for over two hundred years.

INFLATABLE BUILDINGS. Large-scale inflatable structures rely on air pressure that is constantly maintained by blowers. The portability of such structures makes them appropriate for emergencies and temporary events.

TUBING. Inner tubes are torus-shaped balloons made from an airtight material. An inner tube is placed inside a tire and inflated with air to give the tire its final shape and firmness. Used recreationally for tubing on water or snow, old inner tubes are well-suited to holding the human body.

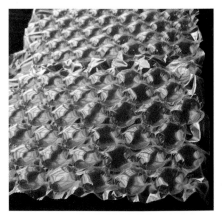

INFLATABLE PACKING. The air pockets in Bubble Wrap reduce material and shipping costs because they occupy space without significantly increasing the weight of the package. Some packaging is inflated on-demand, reducing the need to store air.

LATEX BALLOONS ARE MADE BY DIPPING A CERAMIC OR GLASS SHAPE INTO LIQUID RUBBER.

BALLOON LAMP. This energy-saving lamp, shown here in a cluster formation as well as solitary, is made with a rubber balloon and LED technology. The user inflates the balloon, minimizing packaging. Unlike incandescent lamps, the LED doesn't give off heat. It conserves energy while delivering high illumination over a long lifetime. Design: Kouichi Okamoto.

There are two basic ways to prototype inflatable structures: make them *look* like inflatables, or make them *work* like inflatables. An RF (radio frequency) welding machine is used to manufacture inflatables. To make a simple prototype, use plastic sheets and an iron or bag sealer to weld the plastic. You can also fake this process by making a sewn structure and stuffing it with polyfill (pillow stuffing).

WINE BAGS are leakproof vessels equipped with an airtight valve. Here, they have been washed and filled with air, becoming an intriguing material for new experiments. Think about what you could make with them.

KELSYUS FLOATING LOUNGER uses a twist-fold structural frame and inflatable inserts to create both structure and buoyancy. (See Rods and Tubes for more information on twist-fold structures.) Nylon fabric on the outside holds the elements together. Using both inflatable and twist-fold structures significantly minimizes the material used. Design: Kelsyus.

LARGE VALVE. Deflating takes time, and who wants to spend extra time packing up after a day at the beach? This safe but oversized valve makes the job faster.

PROTOTYPING TECHNIQUES

TRAPPED AIR GIVES STRUCTURE TO INFLATABLES. THE SHAPE AND ARRANGEMENT OF THE AIR POCKETS AFFECT HOW THE OBJECT WILL BEHAVE. USE THE AIR CHAMBERS TO CREATE FOLDABLE OR RIGID STRUCTURES.

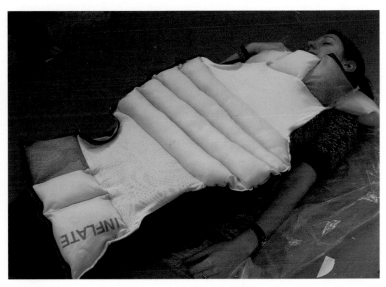

COMMUNICATING WITH GRAPHICS is important in an emergency situation. Bold graphics printed on the vest communicate the steps of transforming the blanket into a safety vest.

STUFFED POCKETS. The designer simulated an inflatable structure by sewing and stuffing pockets. In this prototype, multiple vests link together to create a blanket or shelter. An earlier mock-up was created from Bubble Wrap. Closed cell foam and other small inflatable objects can be used to test the buoyancy of the inflatable. Design: Meredith McFall and Marnay Harris, MICA.

SEALING PLASTIC with a kitchen bag sealer is a method for prototyping inflatable structures. Leave a small hole for pumping in the air. When the bag is filled with air, seal the opening.

STUFFED PINCUSHION was designed to look like an inflatable object. Filled with polyester instead of air, it will not deflate when stuck with pins and needles. Design: Inna Alesina for Kikkerland.

LEATHER

Leather is a natural material created from animal skin via age-old techniques as well as evolving industrial methods. Leather is made from fish as well as from reptiles and land animals; salmon leather comes from waste reclaimed from the canning industry. Tanning is a chemical process that prevents skin from decaying and breaking down, converting it into a durable and versatile surface. Various tanning processes yield different kinds of leather, from a soft, supple skin to a hard, solid substance. Commonly used as a surface, leather can also be cut into broad straps and thin strips. Laser-cutting and engraving are used to make leather jewelry and accessories. Wet leather is pliable and slippery; leather hardens as it dries.

Every piece of leather is unique, and different areas within a single skin may respond in different ways to processes such as carving, shaping, and dyeing. Leather hardened by heat and pressure will retain its form almost indefinitely. It can be colored with paints and dyes to yield rich colors.

FLEXIBLE SURFACE. Cuts made in the outer layer of these shoes allow the surface to bend while creating a seamless perforated skin. Design: Nike.

DRUMS are made by stretching wet leather over a rigid frame. The leather tightens when it dries.

THE SPLIT SEAT is made of vegetable-tanned leather, which acquires structural integrity when soaked in boiling water and dried. The stool is composed of three identical pieces that are sewn together after the hardening process. The rigid leather balances comfort and sturdiness. The cuts in the leather provide some elasticity, minimize material usage, and provide visual interest. Design: Isao Takezawa, RISD.

LEATHER CAN BE SEWN LIKE FABRIC, CARVED LIKE LINOLEUM, CUT LIKE PAPER, SHAPED LIKE METAL, LAMINATED LIKE WOOD, TIED LIKE ROPE, AND KNITTED LIKE YARN. IT CAN BE STRETCHED, COMPRESSED, MOLDED, TOOLED, INLAID, AND MADE TRANSLUCENT OR OPAQUE. LEATHER HAS SUMPTUOUS TEXTURES THAT ARE IMPROVED BY POLISHING AND TREATING WITH PRESERVATIVE AGENTS.

BELT CHAIR. Old belts were used to create the surface of this chair. The frame, made from bent metal tubing, has welded attachments so the belts can be removed and worn. Design: Simona Uzaite, MICA. Photo: Dan Meyers.

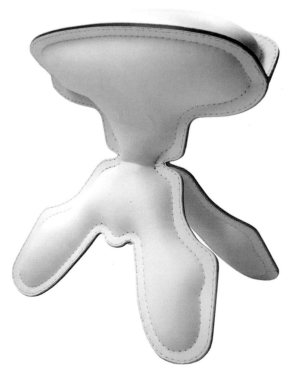

LOST & FOUND. This stool, made from high-density polyurethane foam and leather, was fabricated with a heavy-duty shoe stitching machine. The designer was interested in the simple and honest way that shoemakers construct three-dimensional shapes from flat pieces of leather. Visible stitching reveals the method of construction and provides decorative detail. Although the object has a soft appearance, it is firm like the sole of a shoe. Design: Demakersvan. Photo: Raoul Kramer.

MESH

Mesh is made in many ways from a variety of materials. Each type of mesh has its own behavior. Wire screens on windows and mosquito netting are designed to keep insects at bay. On a larger scale, chicken wire and chain-link fences are meshes used to make strong transparent barriers. Mesh is also used in the medical field in reconstructive surgeries. Minimal, flexible, and strong, mesh provides a hidden structure to living tissues as well as to industrial materials like concrete. The shape of mesh (diamond or square) affects its behavior.

KITCHEN STRAINER. Mesh is commonly used as a filter.

MESH SUPPORTS THE USER'S BODY without traditional foam and fabric. The seating surface of the Aeron chair, designed by Bill Stumpf and Don Chadwick for Herman Miller, Inc., is made from an elastomeric suspension fabric called Pellicle®, manufactured by The Quantum Group. Photo courtesy of Herman Miller.

ON-DEMAND VENT opens with a pull of a cord for maximum athletic performance. During a training run, some athletes shed layers when they get hot. This technology allows the user to open a large area of the shell for immediate cooling. Design: 180s.

DESIGNERS USE WOVEN MESH IN A VARIETY OF SCALES, FROM FINE-GRAINED FILTERS USED IN MEDICINE TO LARGE-APERTURED SURFACES FOR FURNITURE AND BUILDINGS.

CANASTA. Designer Patricia Urquiola has borrowed a technique from traditional woven rattan work to create furniture with oversized strips of polyethylene. Photo courtesy of B&B Italia.

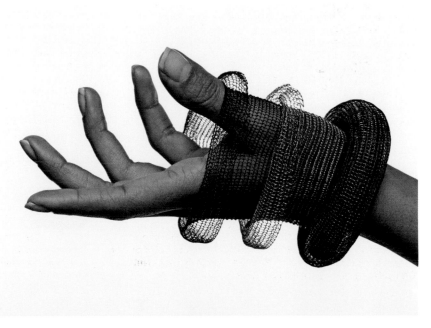

MESH bracelet consists of two layers of knitted copper wire threads. The bracelet has a light, translucent structure with shimmering colors and a glossy reflective surface. The bracelet can be worn rolled-up or lightly unrolled like a cuff. Design: Lisbeth Dauv. Photo: Jeppe Gudmundsen Holmgreen.

Mesh can be woven or stamped, flexible or rigid, 2D or 3D, virtual or real. It is often transparent, a characteristic that adds to its visual beauty as well as its function as a permeable barrier or filter.

STAMPED/MOLDED MESH is highly stable. Made from metal or plastic, it can be used for packaging or to reinforce other materials.

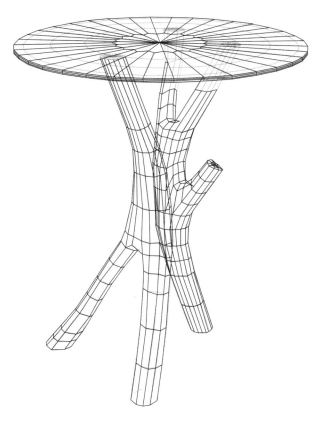

WIRE FRAME for 3D computer model employs a virtual mesh structure. Design: Sara Rossbach, MICA.

PATTERN PLAY. Place one piece of mesh on top of another and shift slightly. You will see a dizzying pattern known as a moiré. Lighting designers use overlapping screens to create different lighting effects.

PROTOTYPING TECHNIQUES

EXPERIMENT WITH MANUFACTURED MESHES, OR CREATE YOUR OWN MESH BY CUTTING AND KNOTTING STRING, WIRE, PLASTIC, AND OTHER MATERIALS.

SHAPED FRUIT BOWL was made by dipping metal mesh into rubber. Design: Martin Konrad Gloeckle.

MODIFYING EXISTING PRODUCTS. See what you can make from an inexpensive mesh laundry basket. To make a compound surface with stretch mesh, you need to create channels for the new structure. Here, we constructed channels by sewing a binding and leaving an opening to insert a wire. Design: Inna Alesina.

FASTEN OBJECTS TOGETHER by weaving them through the cells of a piece of mesh.

TIE SIMPLE KNOTS to make your own mesh.

The cells in diamond-shaped mesh are designed to collapse, allowing the surface to change shape during use. Dynamic diamond mesh commonly is found in packaging, hammocks, stockings, and other products whose surface conforms to a body or object inside it.

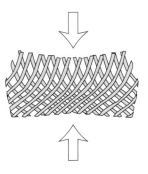

MESH DEFORMS when pushed or pulled in different directions.

EXTRUDED MESH is used for grocery packaging. It is flexible and will take the shape of the object it encases.

EXTRUDED POLYPROPYLENE MESH makes a useful bath sponge. The texture lathers the soap while the open cells and slippery material prevent the growth of bacteria.

EXPANDED MESH is made by making cuts in a flat material and pulling it apart, yielding a textured surface.

KNOTTED OR WOVEN MESH is an ancient material still used today for hammocks and fishing nets.

DIAMOND MESH HAS A HELIX SHAPE THAT IS BOTH FUNCTIONAL AND VISUALLY ENGAGING.

ORANGE AND LEMON TREE LIGHTS use plastic netting for both structure and decoration. This strong, inexpensive material is commonly used for packing fruits and vegetables. The netting diffuses light while providing a hanging device. It partially conceals the electrical cord, addressing a basic problem in the design of pendant lights. Embracing its original role as a packing material, the netting also serves to package the light. Design: Suhyun Hwang.

MINIMAL STRUCTURE. The Kaktus stool is made from cast aluminum. It takes inspiration from the fibrous skeleton of the staghorn cholla cactus. This lightweight stool can support considerable weight. Here, the diagonal forms are visually dynamic but physically fixed. Design: Enrico Bressan for Artecnica Inc.

Braided mesh is used in many industrial applications. Available in tubular, flat, or cordage forms, this material is employed in cables, shoelaces, and water hoses, and as a base for composite structures. Fiber types and weaving methods can be varied within a single braided material. Because the fibers are woven, the braid can deform. In the toy known as a Chinese finger trap, tightening occurs when the braid is pulled; because the total surface area of the braid remains constant, the trap loses diameter to gain length. This dynamic behavior appears in various braided materials.

Collapsible scissor structures are another variation of the dynamic diamond mesh form. This simple mechanism is used in many products that are designed to adjust and change shape.

KNOTTY LACES provide custom tension control by temporarily restricting the movement of the lace through the shoe's eyelets. How does it work? The lace's elastic core is enclosed in a braided sleeve whose braiding helix is different in the knotted and unknotted sections. When the elastic is pulled, the knots collapse; when the elastic is released, the knots reappear, holding the laces in place. Design: Mike Gonzalez, Xtenex.

TUBULAR BRAIDS are used as cable sleeves, fire hoses, and shoelaces.

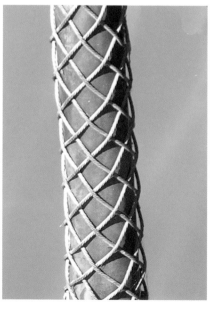

WIRE MESH PULLING GRIPS support a cable's weight as it hangs.

A COLLAPSIBLE SCISSOR STRUCTURE, WHICH HAS MANY FAMILIAR USES, IS ESSENTIALLY A STRUCTURAL DIAMOND MESH.

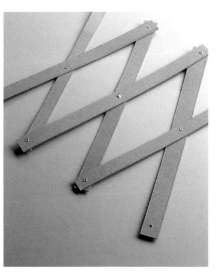

CARDBOARD SCISSOR STRUCTURE. Rivets or bolts can connect lengths of material at key pivot points to construct an adjustable surface. Here, we used rivets and non-corrugated cardboard.

SCISSOR STRUCTURES are used for folding gates and other collapsible structures.

DESKTOP DIVIDER. This file organizer is made from stainless steel.

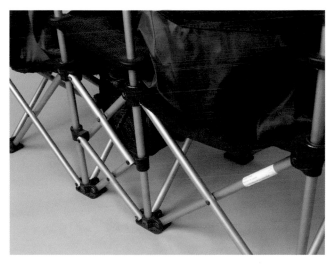

FOLDING CHAIRS commonly use steel or aluminum tubes as structural members. In this chair, the diagonal sections slide along the vertical members. Special plastic hardware has been designed to hold the elements together and allow them to slide.

PAPER

The word *paper* refers to the ancient Egyptian writing material papyrus, which was formed from beaten strips of papyrus plants. Paper consists of fibers that are soaked in water and then drained through a mesh surface; the fibers fuse via hydrogen bonding into a stable flat material. Wood pulp is the most common source of fibers for contemporary papermaking. Cotton and linen are the basis of high-quality rag paper. Although paper is commonly used for printing and communication, it has many uses in product design. In China, paper umbrellas were invented to provide shade from the sun and were later waxed and lacquered to provide protection from rain. Paper can be folded into complex 3D objects with dynamic properties. It can be laminated to create finishing materials such as Formica. Wastepaper can be recovered and made into other materials and products, generally of a lower quality (down-cycling).

EXPANDED PAPER MESH is a cushioning material for wrapping and shipping fragile objects.

WAXED. Paper absorbs water, but it can be waterproofed with wax.

AIR CIRCULATION. This insulating jacket for a coffee cup is an improvement from corrugated cardboard sleeves because it uses only one material. (Corrugated board consists of two glued layers.) Making this product from unbleached recycled paper would be even better.

PAPER IS MORE THAN A FLAT SURFACE FOR WRITING AND PRINTING. IT CAN BE SHREDDED, FOLDED, PERFORATED, WOVEN, AND FOLDED INTO MANY SURPRISING OBJECTS.

Designers use paper in many unexpected ways. Paper structures and furniture are made by compressing shredded waste into shapes. Sheets of paper are cut and layered to create structural and decorative objects. Paper-folding techniques based on origami can be revisited to create functional objects and wall coverings. Old newspapers can be cut and wound into yarn and woven into rugs and other objects. Easy to work with and available for free from the nearby recycling bin, paper is a versatile and inspiring material.

BALES OF PAPER. Paper is packed into large bales during the recycling process. Here, the industrial harvest is used in an exhibition. Design: FLUX Studio with Gensler.

IPOD COVER. An iPod is stored in a cavity cut out from the interior of a used sketch book. Design: Micah Spear, MICA.

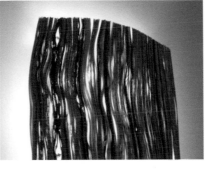

WALL LIGHTS. Reclaimed paper has been shredded and glued to make a lampshade. Design: Inna Alesina.

COLORED PAPER. Disks of wound paper were sprayed with dye. The edges of the shredded paper accept the color well.

Fiber rush is an inexpensive artificial wicker material made from tightly twisted strips of craft paper. Twisting strengthens the material. Natural rush is made from the leaves of cattails, bullrush, and other plants. It is labor-intensive to produce.

SIT TEXTILE FURNITURE Made from Finnish paper twine, this hand-knitted seat was inspired by the nest of the weaver bird. The object consists of untreated fiber rush. Design: Tine Kirkemann Heuser.

WOVEN RUSH is strong and beautiful. Many people don't realize that rush is often made of paper.

Shopping bag handles are cheap and strong. They use the same underlying material as the shopping bag (kraft paper), structured in a different way (fiber rush).

LAMP SHADES EXPLOIT PAPER'S ABILITY TO DIFFUSE LIGHT. CONSIDER
POSSIBILITIES BEYOND THE OBVIOUS.

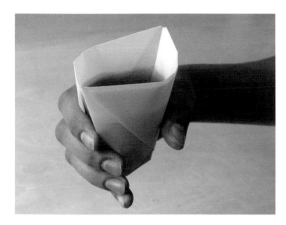

ORIGAMI CUP. A single sheet of paper can be folded into
a waterproof vessel. The cup must be held in a certain
way to function.

ORIGAMI SHADE. This light shade is made of many
origami paper cups attached together. During a party,
guests are invited to pull off cups and use them,
changing the light quality as the party progresses.
Design: Olivia Peralta and Hilary Siber, MICA.

SLIDE FOLD. By folding and connecting individual pieces
of paper, the designer created a surface that can be used
as a screen or a textured wall covering. To connect the
long strips of material into a larger surface, the designer
cut the joints in half in certain places so that the lengths could be staggered and
hooked together. The joints at these staggered points of connection are weaker
than elsewhere. Design: Nick Henninger, Auburn University.

DISCARDED PHONE BOOKS were used to create a soft and comfortable seating surface. Design: Inna Alesina.

ROUNDED EDGES of reclaimed printed pages are crafted into the shape of a vase with an aluminum core.

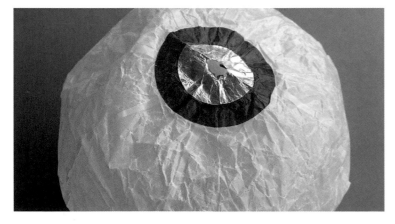

INFLATABLE PAPER BALL. Pieces of paper have been glued together to form a sphere. The ball holds its shape when inflated, thanks to the structural properties of paper. Design: Georg Baldele.

PAPER UMBRELLAS unfold to offer protection from sun and rain.

EMBOSSING, DEBOSSING, PRINTING, WATERPROOFING, LASER CUTTING, GLUING, AND STITCHING ARE JUST A FEW TECHNIQUES EMPLOYED IN WORKING WITH PAPER.

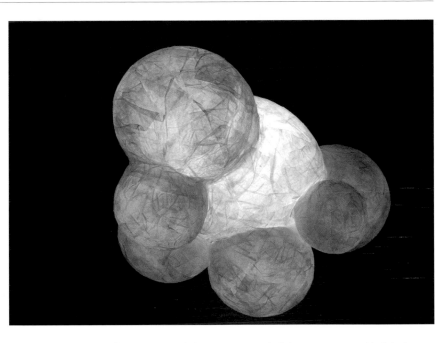

FILTER LIGHT. This light fixture was made by wrapping and gluing paper around inflated balloons. When the structure dried, the balloons were popped and removed. Wiring was inserted to complete the fixture. Design: Mike Reynolds, MICA.

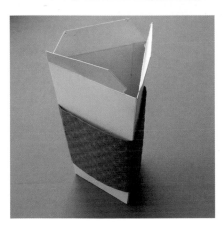

PAPER CUP WITH INTEGRATED LID aims to eliminate the waste created by the two-part design of a disposable paper cup and plastic lid. Design: Nicholas Richardson, MICA.

LEAN PLATE. This prototype for a paper plate liner is designed to absorb grease from foods. Grease makes the paper translucent, revealing a hidden image on the other side of the liner. Design: Inna Alesina and Sharon Zohar Gil.

PAPER PULP

Made primarily from recycled paper, molded paper pulp is cheap, durable, resilient, and environmentally friendly. Molded fiber is used for packaging and egg cartons, and for the end caps used inside boxes to cushion fragile objects. Recently, designers have started using this humble material in more visible ways, employing it for shelving, booster seats, biodegradable flower pots, disposable tableware, and more. It can be shaped into myriad complex and functional forms.

BAJA BBQ FIREPACK features a 100% recycled biodegradable paper pulp package that is burned along with the charcoal inside; no lighter fuel is required. The package also serves as a chimney. Design: Mike and Maaike for Design Annex/Lazzari.

DISPOSABLE FOOD CONTAINERS. Ordinary objects can be a great source of inspiration for designers. All the cutouts, hinges, and protrusions of a cardboard egg carton are molded in a single step; note the handy locking mechanism. Fruit trays are durable enough to be reused many times and can eventually be recycled.

MOLDED PAPER PULP CAN TAKE MANY SHAPES, BUT IT WILL ALWAYS HAVE A SOFT, ORGANIC CHARACTER.

ACOUSTICART. These tiles are designed to perfectly tessellate, providing an intriguing surface that absorbs sound. Suitable for covering an entire wall, the tiles can also be used to construct free-floating shapes. The tiles are made from 100% recycled paper with natural additives. Design: Giulia Longo, Natural Mente Design.

MOLDED PAPER COMPOSITE BOARD. This material was made by mixing Elmer's glue with paper pulp and squeezing out excess water by hand. The mixture was then pressed into wooden molds. The outer mold was removed, and the pieces were dried in a gas kiln. They were sanded after drying. Design: Laura Keller, Auburn University.

Handmade paper is not the first material people think of for making computers. Yet designers today are looking for innovative ways to embed technology into unexpected materials. In this way a team at the MIT Media Lab mixed low-tech craft with high technology.

FIBER SOUP. Paper fibers are mixed with water and broken down with a beater. The broken fibers are strained through a thin nylon mesh to remove water and form a sheet. Design: Marcelo Coelho, MIT Media Lab; Joanna Berzowska and Lyndl Hall, XS Labs.

BUILDING A SURFACE. Larger paper sheets are made by overlapping smaller ones on top of each other. The fibers shrink as they dry, fusing the sheets together.

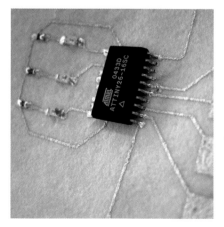

INSIDE THE PAPER SANDWICH. Electronic components and a printed circuit board are placed on top of a paper sheet. A second sheet is layered on top to fully encapsulate the components.

THE OUTER SURFACE. Embedded elements, including LED lights, printed conductors, and controls, remain visible through the paper's translucent surface.

FLEXIBLE SENSOR. Resistive inks are used to make this paper-based sensor. When the paper bends, the resistance of the ink changes and can be measured electronically. This type of technology could be used for making books whose pages know when they are turned, or boxes that sense their weight and stress, or interactive origami.

PROTOTYPING TECHNIQUES

MAKE YOUR OWN MOLDED PULP WITH BASIC KITCHEN TOOLS.

MAKE PULP. After experimenting with discarded molded packaging, we tried making our own pulp. We soaked old newspapers in hot water. With a blender from a thrift store, we blended the wet paper with more water.

REMOVE WATER. We removed water with a colander and then squeezed out more water by hand. If you don't remove the excess water, the resulting object will dry too slowly; the material will be thick but the object will be too light and will not be strong enough.

MOLD THE PULP. We pressed the pulp against a variety of screens. We experimented with an old rattan rocker, woven baskets, a dryer lint trap, and a metal screen.

PAPER DOME. This object was made by pressing pulp against a wire backet. Object study: Inna Alesina.

Filler flats are a special type of egg crate packaging. Designed for holding thirty eggs, they nest for storage and are used in restaurants and for high-volume food service. They typically are not recycled, as they are made from third-generation recycled paper with a high level of impurities.

We were curious about the possibilities of this intriguing structural material. Collecting them was a difficult job by itself, as most users considered them to be waste. Furthermore, we needed our egg crates to all be the same kind (there are several variations on the design) so that they would nest without ugly gaps. We found a warehouse that was collecting crates to sell back to farms at a low price, so we were able to get a lot of postconsumer egg crates.

We cut the crates on a band saw and experimented with the nesting pieces to create a simple stool with a rich texture.

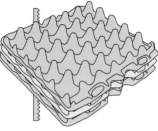

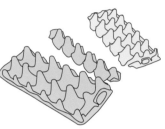

1. CUT. Stack a few pieces and cut egg crates on a band saw to make one narrow piece and two wide pieces.

2. SEPARATE. Separate narrow and wide pieces into two different stacks.

3. NEST. You will have twice as many wide pieces as narrow ones, so nest one narrow piece between two wide pieces.

CUT AND COLOR. After cutting and nesting pieces, we sprayed them with water-based dye and allowed them to air dry. We created patterns by assembling different colors. The process is like weaving.

BUILDING A CURVE. The layers of material naturally hold together. To make a curve, we inserted one wide piece between every two narrow pieces.

DESIGNERS LOVE TO FIND NEW USES FOR ORDINARY MATERIALS.

ASSEMBLY. The stacked materials curve to form a donut shape.

CLAMPING IT TOGETHER. We used a canvas clamp to tighten the circle. This part requires strong muscles and needs to be done slowly. Tightening it too quickly can damage the paper edges.

FINAL SHAPE. When the final shape is achieved, the entire object is secured with plastic straps and crimped. This experimental double roll consists of two concentric rings of material. The piece serves as a small stool or ottoman. Design: Inna Alesina.

PLASTIC, BIO

Conventional plastic food packaging, including polystyrene, polyethylene terephthalate, polypropylene, and Styrofoam, requires a lot of energy to produce and is typically made from petroleum. Biodegradable plastics are derived from plants, animals, and microorganisms. They generate no off-gassing hazards, and they rely on renewable resources. Bioplastics made from corn, wheat, or sugarcane are widely used in packaging.

However, bioplastics are not a magic bullet for the world's environmental and economic woes. Converting the food supply into plastic and fuel contributes to global food shortages. Many biodegradable materials require access to oxygen in order to break down, while landfills usually provide anaerobic conditions. Like any material, bioplastic has both benefits and drawbacks.

COMPOSTABLE BUT SLOW. Containers and cold drink cups made from NatureWorks biopolymers will biodegrade into CO_2 and water in an industrial anaerobic composting facility, where specific levels of heat and moisture are maintained; the process takes about forty-seven days. We tried composting cups at home in an ordinary compost area and saw no signs of decomposition after two months.

MOLDED WALL PANELS. In this experimental project, a bioplastic material was concocted from water, glycerin, gelatin, and food coloring and was molded into wall panels.

A series of discarded parabolic light panels (8 x 13 inches) served as molds. Wires were embedded in the liquid plastic to support and connect the wall for final assembly.

Design: Jennifer Thompson, Auburn University. Photos: Magdalena Garmaz and Jennifer Thompson.

NEW PLASTICS MADE FROM PLANT MATERIAL OFFER A LOT OF PROMISE. DESIGNERS, ENGINEERS, AND SCIENTISTS ARE WORKING TO CREATE NEW MATERIALS THAT WORK BETTER FOR PEOPLE AND THE PLANET.

HOMEMADE PLASTIC. Most designers are not chemists; the experiments shown here came from the designer's kitchen. She gathered every kind of starch she could find, including tapioca, soy, green bean, potato, and corn, and added natural fibers for structural purposes. She tried cooking, baking, frying, microwaving, and air and sun drying to find a workable technique. After several months of trial and error, she created compostable food packaging that communicates the freshness of the product inside. Design: Hyeshin Kim, MICA.

PLASTIC FILM

Plastic film is used in shopping bags, trash bags, and protective wrap for food and objects. Although 38 percent of all packaging consists of plastic film, only 6 percent gets recycled, and most of that is turned into plastic lumber, a down-cycled product. The various resins and colors in plastic film make it difficult to recycle. Most plastic film is a virgin material containing little or no postconsumer waste; about five million tons are incinerated or landfilled each year. Compared with many other packaging materials, plastic film is beneficial because it does its work with a very thin surface. The vast amounts that are consumed, however, make it a burden on the environment.

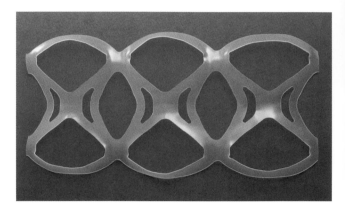

CHEAP BUT DANGEROUS. Six-pack rings are hazardous to animals when released into the environment. Inventing an alternative is a good challenge for designers.

MINIMAL PACKAGE. Milk bags are commonly used internationally, but not in the United States. The package has no structure; the user places it in a special pitcher and cuts the corner to pour. Made from a single material, the bag is suitable for recycling.

ANTISTATIC BAG for electronics has a special finish to protect sensitive electronic components and computer boards from electrostatic discharge during handling, shipping, and assembly.

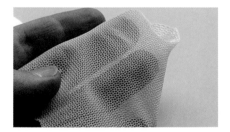

BREATHABLE. This skin like surface (top) is the upper layer of a feminine pad. Perforated bags from the grocery store (bottom) sometimes feature slits and/or holes that let air through and preserve produce longer.

PLASTIC FILM IS A THIN, MINIMAL MATERIAL THAT IS USUALLY THROWN AWAY AFTER USE. IT HAS MANY POSSIBILITIES BEYOND SHIPPING AND PACKAGING.

Plastic films that shrink when exposed to heat are commonly used in retail packaging. Shrink film is also a shipping material employed for bundling and protecting loads. Bundling films are thicker, softer, and cloudier than the brilliantly clear shrink films used in retail packaging. These films have intriguing applications for designers and hobbyists as well.

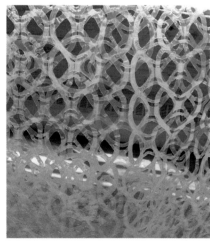

FLAT WATERING CAN. Some objects nest for storage or shipping, but this watering pouch is completely flat until it is filled with water. Two handles help in maneuvering the shape.

INSTANT GREENHOUSE. We used ordinary kitchen wrap to make a small greenhouse by wrapping an old table frame. Design: Inna Alesina.

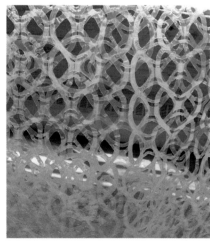

PLASTIC LACE. This lace like surface was created by fusing six-pack rings with an iron. Design: Benjamin Howard, MICA.

POLY IKAT TAPE is a strong, flexible material from Japan designed for use in resist dying (like tie-dyeing). It splits easily into strips as small as 1/16-inch wide. It has many potential uses, such as weaving a minimal net to carry large objects.

Fusing objects between layers of low-density polyethylene (used to make shopping bags) creates new possibilities for constructing objects. Try experimenting with mesh, lace, and other plastic objects. Magnets and other features can be embedded when fusing the sheets together.

OUTSOURCED PROTOTYPES. These prototypes of plastic bladders filled with liquid would be impossible to create without RF (radio frequency) welding technology. We created vector files in Adobe Illustrator and sent specs to a sample maker, who made these realistic, water-tight pouches. The prototypes are for a kitchen system called PacRac, designed to save countertop space and dispense liquids such as dish soap, olive oil, vegetable oil, and vinegar. The push-button valve also functions as a hook. Design: Zoe Axelrod, Steven McNamara, and Gregory Murphy, MICA.

PLASTIC FASHION BAGS. These totes were made by fusing several layers of plastic bags with mesh, yarn, and other structural materials to create durable and waterproof surfaces. The bags were assembled with a sewing machine. Design: Ricci Brigantti, Columbia College, Chicago.

CREATE NEW MATERIAL by fusing several plastic bags together. Place a sheet of waxed paper or tracing paper on a protected surface. Lay down a plastic bag and then your mesh or other materials. Add another plastic bag and another piece of smooth paper. Iron the area on a low setting. Let your work cool and then peel off both sheets of paper.

WHEN IS A BAG NOT A BAG? THE CHARACTERISTICS THAT MAKE PLASTIC FILM SUCH A COMPELLING PACKAGING MATERIAL CAN ALSO BE APPLIED TO PRODUCT DESIGN: STRENGTH, LIGHTNESS, DURABILITY, ECONOMY, AND TRANSPARENCY.

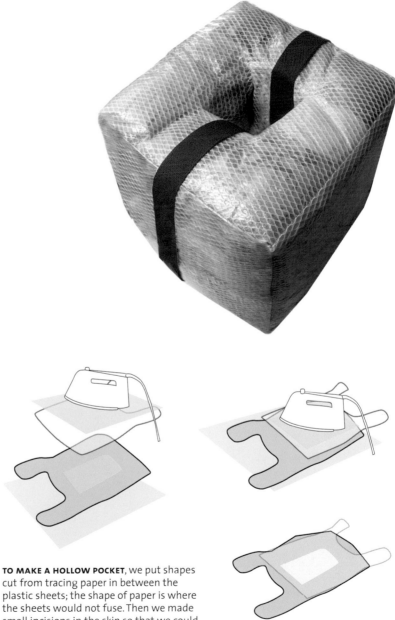

FUSED CUBE. This furniture module was made from a plastic skin stuffed with reclaimed plastic bags, which become structural when compressed. The outer skin was created by fusing nylon mesh between two layers of LDPE plastic film (from shopping bags) with an iron. Smaller units were used to fill the large unit. The completed cube can attach to other cubes with a strap to construct any type of furniture. Design: Inna Alesina.

TO MAKE A HOLLOW POCKET, we put shapes cut from tracing paper in between the plastic sheets; the shape of paper is where the sheets would not fuse. Then we made small incisions in the skin so that we could remove the paper and insert stuffing to make 3D structures.

PLASTIC, MOLDED

Injection blow molding is a common industrial technique for producing large numbers of hollow objects in glass or plastic. The material is inflated inside a "preform." The preform includes the necks of the bottles and the threads or "finish" as well as the volume of the hollow object. Bottles, containers, and other products are manufactured this way.

UBIQUITOUS. All plastic bottles, from eye-drop containers to gallon milk jugs, are made by blow molding.

DIY BLOW MOLDING. Designer Jim Termeer has experimented by hand with techniques similar to industrial blow molding. His Daisy vase is made from a plastic Bic pen. Part of the pen is heated on a flame and hand blown, creating a new object.

The bottom of the vase is formed by filling the bulb with water and then shaping it against a metal form. Design and photo: Jim Termeer for giffin'termeer.

LIGHT, SHINY, AND COLORFUL, PLASTIC BECAME THE DEFINING MATERIAL OF THE TWENTIETH CENTURY.

Melamine resin is a hard plastic made from melamine and formaldehyde. This material is often used in kitchen implements and plates. It also commonly serves as a finishing material; paper impregnated with melamine resin is laminated onto particle board to create surfaces for cabinets, shelving, and furniture.

HARD CANDY. Melamine is a popular material for bright kitchen implements.

PAINTED PROTOTYPE of stacked Lollie plates. Design: Iduol Beny.

UNIFIED AND UNIQUE. Lollie plates were designed using 3D modeling software and rapid prototyping tools. The final design could be executed in melamine. A section of a computer-generated model helps the designer to see how each plate stacks.

PLASTIC PUZZLE. Digital rendering shows how the Lollie plates stack together to make a solid.

Rotational molding uses heat and biaxial rotation (rotation on two axes) to produce hollow, one-piece objects. The chocolate rabbits sold at Easter are rotomolded: the melted chocolate is swirled around inside the mold to create a big, hollow form. Rotomolding is slower than injection molding, where parts can be made in a few seconds, but rotational molds are much cheaper to make than injection molds. A large object such as a kayak or plastic trash bin can be manufactured inexpensively and with minimal waste using this process.

ROTOMOLDING. Kayaks are made by rotational molding. The process makes it possible to mold large hollow objects.

IMAGINE that this empty bottle is a mold and the blue paint inside is a polymer powder. The mold is heated while it is rotated. The liquid polymer adheres to the walls. Finally, after cooling, the mold is removed, resulting in a hollow blue plastic bottle.

Extrusion and protrusion are used to create long, continuous forms with a fixed cross-sectional profile by pushing or pulling material through a die. Metals, polymers, ceramics, and pasta are all commonly extruded materials. The process can be performed on hot or cold materials, and it yields a consistent surface finish. Products made this way include pipes, tracks, wires, and railings.

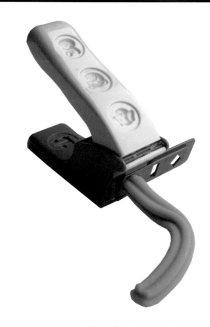

EXTRUSION. Spaghetti, macaroni, and drinking straws are all extruded through a die.

PLAY DOH MACHINES use the extrusion principle, pushing material through a small aperture.

MAKING A SILICONE MOLD IS SIMILAR (IN IDEA) TO MAKING A MOLD FOR INJECTION MOLDING.

Injection molding forces molten plastic at high pressure into a precisely machined mold made of steel or aluminum. Injection molding is used to manufacture everything from tiny toys and small machine parts to the bodies of cars and appliances. The mold is expensive to engineer and tool, so this method is reserved for high-volume production.

COMMONPLACE. Most solid plastic objects in your home are injection molded.

PROTOTYPING TECHNIQUES

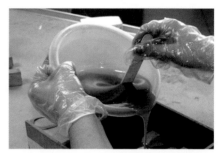

MAKING A SILICONE MOLD. A wooden master matches the object to be cast. Petroleum jelly is carefully brushed onto the master. The master is clayed up with a special clay (Klean Klay) to define the parting line between the halves of the mold. Keys are made to ensure perfect alignment of the two halves. Next, mixed silicone is poured into the master. Use protective clothing, a respirator, and good ventilation.

When both halves of the silicone mold are cured, they are taped and clamped together so that the actual object can be poured. The multiple shown here is cast from plaster.

PLASTIC SHEET

Plastic sheets are used to make cartons, cups, coffee lids, and other products. This material comes in different thicknesses and hardnesses and in plastics with various behaviors and chemical properties. Thermoformed plastics are made by heating a plastic sheet and shaping it over a mold. The molds are inexpensive to tool and engineer and have a fast turnaround time, making this a common technique for prototyping and for short-run manufacturing. In vacuum forming, one of the most common thermoforming processes, the heated sheet is sucked against the mold as air is drawn out of the mold chamber. Big plastic objects such as thin-walled car bumpers can be made by thermoforming a plastic sheet; so can small objects such as museum clips.

IMPORTANT NUMBERS. The two berry packages shown here look the same, but they are made from different materials. Although both are made by the vacuum-forming process, the strawberries are packaged in polystyrene and the blueberries in PET. In many parts of the United States, polyethylene terephthalate (PET) packaging can be recycled, while polystyrene will be either landfilled or incinerated. The numbers inside the chasing arrows indicate different kinds of plastic suitable for different modes of disposal. PET packaging (number 1) is preferable.

SOLO COFFEE LID is made from two thermoformed pieces that lock together. The drinking spout can be slid open and closed for safety, eliminating the tear-open feature of many previous designs.

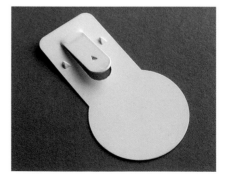

DIE-CUT PLASTIC. On the back of this museum clip, you can see the simple die-cut mechanism designed to secure the clip to the wearer's clothing.

PLASTIC SHEETS ARE USED TO MAKE 3D SHAPES AS WELL AS FLAT SURFACES. LASER CUTTING, LASER ETCHING, AND DIE-CUTTING ARE USED FOR PROTOTYPING AND PRODUCING OBJECTS FROM PLASTIC SHEETS.

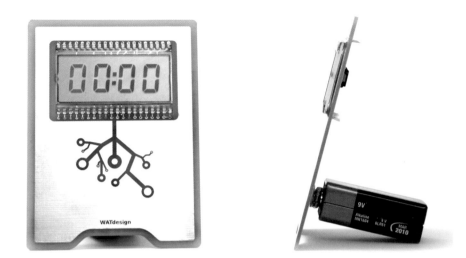

ZER00:00 is a low-tech digital clock, consisting only of a battery and a printed circuit board with LCD and timer. The battery serves as a stand, and the etching is a decorative element. The designers used standard techniques for etching circuit boards—which are normally not seen by consumers—to create the clock face. Design: WAT Design, Jan Habraken, Maarten Baptist, and Jos Kranen.

PRECISION LASER CUTTING. Malebag and iPod clip are products made from clear acrylic and cow leather. All the functional features, such as notches for elastic bands and cord and port cutouts, are cut by a laser. The Malebag has an opening for attaching the plastic iPod clip, integrating the two products. Design: Wolf Udo Wagner for MiaWolf.

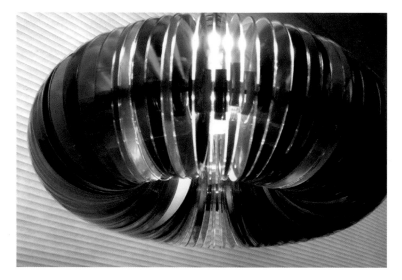

CD LAMP SHADE. The mirror finish and bright graphics of reclaimed CDs can be an asset to a new design. Placing CDs in a microwave oven for a few seconds creates cracked patterns on the foil layer. They are hard to glue, so this design involves threading through their central openings to fasten them together. Rings from plastic bottles were used as spacers. Design: Inna Alesina.

CD WALL. The foil was stripped from CDs with a heat gun and duct tape. Ninety-degree wedges were cut from each CD and heat-formed into pyramids. The resulting shapes were riveted together to make a wall surface. Design: Mona Pedro, Auburn University.

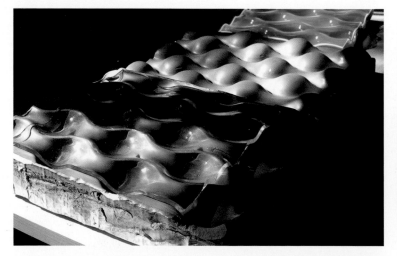

THERMOFORMED ACRYLIC. This fruit tray was inspired by the molded paper trays that protect fruit during shipping. An actual paper tray was used to make male and female Hydrocal plaster molds. A sheet of acrylic was heated in an oven at 220 degrees. When the sheet became soft and pliable, it was sandwiched

between the two plaster molds. After they had cooled for several minutes, the molds were opened and the final object was complete. Design: Inna Alesina.

PROTOTYPING TECHNIQUES

DESIGNERS USE HEAT-FORMED PLASTIC SHEETS TO MAKE MODELS FOR NEW PRODUCTS AND TO SIMULATE VARIOUS PROCESSES.

The plastic was spray-painted to resemble stainless steel. Design: Inna Alesina and Sharon Gil.

TABLEWARE PROTOTYPES. Sheets of acrylic were used to prototype a set of eating utensils. Laser-cut pieces were heated with a heat gun. (You also can use an oven.) To make quick studies, we used existing silverware to shape our plastic, although wooden jigs work better for making consistent multiples. The cutout wedge on the spoon makes it possible to shape the bowl form. Use leather gloves to protect yourself from the heat. Solvents, polishing agents, and other compounds are available for working with plastic. Think of ways to attach plastic mechanically rather than chemically where possible.

VACUUM-FORMING PLASTIC. Wooden shapes are commonly used as molds in vacuum forming. The vacuum-forming machine heats a plastic sheet clipped to a magnetic frame. When the sheet softens, the soft plastic is unclipped and brought down on top of the molds. The vacuum former sucks out air, tightly pulling the plastic around the wooden forms.

We used heavy-duty scissors to cut the shapes. After some sanding and buffing of the edges, we got a convincing prototype of this star-shaped food container for kids. Design: Andrea Dombrowski, MICA.

DIE-CUT NECKLACE uses the shape of each cut piece to connect to the next piece. Colorful placemats from a dollar store were used to make prototypes. Design and photo: Lily Yung.

FOLDABLE GREENHOUSE uses scored and folded plastic sheets to create a transparent structure. The middle section detaches with snaps similar to those used in a standard office binder. Design: Daniel Schipper.

PUNCHED HOLES serve to prototype a colorful surface.

PLASTIC FOLDERS are a good source of colorful flexible plastic for prototypes. The folder itself employs welding, fusing, riveting, and glue as methods of construction. Here, tetra shapes were made by heat-welding plastic folders with a household iron. Design: Sunny Chong, MICA.

PROTOTYPING TECHNIQUES

CUT, SCORE, PUNCH HOLES, AND HEAT-SET PLASTIC OBJECTS TO MAKE PROTOTYPES AND FINISHED PRODUCTS FROM PLASTIC SHEETS.

JEWELRY BEADS FROM PLASTIC BOTTLES. The tops and bottoms of PET soda bottles are cut off to create straight sheets.

The sheets are cut into strips. Using a paper cutter makes this easier, because the plastic is very slippery.

Strips can be decorated with permanent markers or by sanding or scraping what will become the inner side of the bead. Then, rolls are made and secured with twist ties.

Arranged on a reclaimed wrought-iron grill, the parts are placed outside on a hot sunny day. Heat from the sun and radiated heat from the grill is enough to set the shape of the rolls.

The beads were finished into jewelry and small objects like key chains, rings, and pendants. Design: Inna Alesina.

RODS AND TUBES

A rod is any material shaped into a long cylinder. A rod can be rigid or flexible, solid or hollow. Rods are manufactured in many materials, including wood, metal, plastic, and composites such as fiberglass and carbon fiber. Fiberglass rods are made of glass fibers in an epoxy matrix. A solid fiberglass rod is formed by forcing material through a small opening. A hollow rod (tube) is lighter and more flexible than a solid rod. Smaller diameter poles are made by wrapping unidirectional filament tape sheets around a core; the core is later removed. Tubes allow diverse types of inner connectors, such as a bungee cord or smaller tubes. Composite rods and tubes have transformed the way contemporary tension-compression structures such as tents and canopies look and function, yielding lighter, larger, and stronger structures.

FISHING ROD is made from a composite tube. The rod is light, strong, long, and relatively flexible.

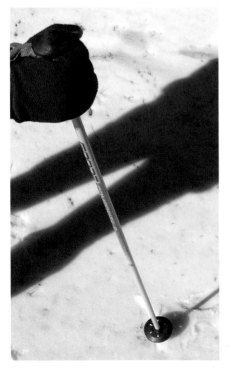

COMPOSITE RODS are used in ski poles and road reflectors.

A TENSION STRUCTURE IS A "FIGHT" BETWEEN FABRIC AND TENSION POLES. THE STRONGER THE POLES, THE TIGHTER THE STRUCTURE, AND THE HARDER IT IS TO SET UP. LONGER POLES ARE MORE FLEXIBLE BUT ALSO FLIMSIER.

BUILDING WITH TENSION. The tents we use today were inspired by the Native American tepee. Native Americans harvested wooden poles on-site from available trees. Collapsible modern tents are made with slightly flexible composite tubes.

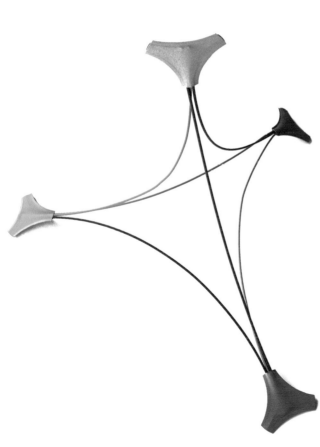

SPACE CLUSTERS KIT is a creative toy that employs slightly flexible plastic rods and connectors to create structures. The special connectors can be used over and over; no scissors or glue is required. As designers, we found this toy useful for modeling rodlike structures, since it is difficult to replicate rod flexibility in a small model. Design: Space Clusters.

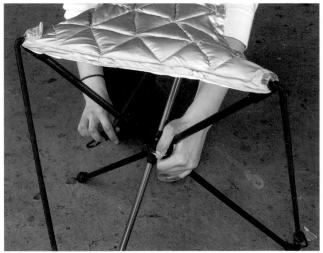

COMPOSITE ADVANTAGE A typical tripod stool uses a pin joint. This one uses tension and stoppers integrated in the composite rod to keep the ring in place.

The designer added hard and soft elements to create a truly composite design. Design: Kallie Sternburgh, MICA.

FLEX. Poles need to flex in order to create a tent structure. Using tube connectors with a preset bend allows the designer to employ stronger poles. Connectors are designed to keep the structure relaxed, and not in tension. Design: Paul Capetola, MICA.

SPRING STEEL. Some smaller twist-fold structures can be made with spring steel bands instead of composite rods. Spring steel is cheaper and more flexible than composite. This spring steel sunshade fits under the windshield to keep the car cool.

PROTOTYPING TECHNIQUES

A COMPOSITE ROD HAS DIRECTIONAL FIBERS. THE SURFACE OF THE ROD IS HARD AND SMOOTH, BUT AT THE ENDS, FINE, SHARP FIBERS CAN COME LOOSE, CREATING A ROUGH SURFACE. THE ROD EASILY SPLITS ALONG THE FIBERS WHEN IT IS PUT UNDER TOO MUCH STRESS.

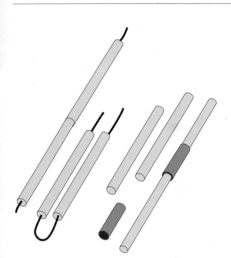

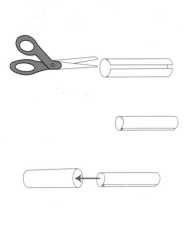

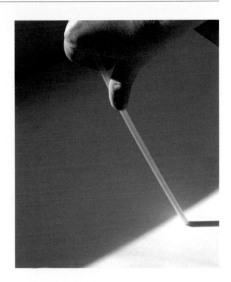

BUNGEE CORD links hollow rods together, making separate short rods work as one long rod. A solid tubular connector is the most effective fastener for rods. Threaded with a bungee cord, the rods make it easy to set up the tent. The rods are then integrated into channels sewn in the tent fabric, distributing the force evenly.

TUBE VERSUS ROD. The properties of a tube are similar to those of a rod, but it is easier to fasten tubes together (as in tent poles, which are strung together). By stuffing a tube with material, you can change its properties, making it perform like a rod. To create a strong rod from a drinking straw,

cut the straw along one side and curl it to a smaller diameter straw. Insert the rolled straw inside a whole straw. Repeat several times until you no longer can insert straws. The resulting object will behave like a rod, but you will still be able to thread string inside it for fastening (like a tube).

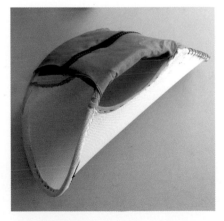

TIP: Roadside reflectors sold at hardware stores are a source for inexpensive composite rods. Designers also use tent poles, plastic or metal hardware, connectors, and clasps from old tents to prototype new structures. Tent poles come in different sizes and levels of flexibility. They are very hard but can be cut with a Dremel cutting wheel. Wear protective clothing, including goggles, gloves, and a respirator, when working with such materials.

FAST PROTOTYPING. Nylon-covered fiberglass cable fishing tape, which is designed for installing communication cables, is useful for prototyping flexible or twist-fold structures. The nylon sheath makes the surface of the rod smooth and safe to work with. It can be cut with a metal saw.

TENSION IN THE ROUND. When you flex a composite rod, it wants to spring back. If you take a long rod and connect it to make a circle, it will want to stay in a circle. This small tension structure was made with flexible fiberglass fishing tape covered with fabric. Design: Inna Alesina.

Thin metal elements are useful for making structures that are both lightweight and strong. Typical uses for metal rods include levers, axles, and drill bits. Drawing metal bars through rollers creates rods that can be machined, forged, or otherwise used for manufacturing a variety of objects. Typically, metal rods are heavier but easier to bend than tubes. Designers have used rebar, meant for reinforcing concrete, to make bent metal structures.

THE AXEL of a folding cart is a metal rod.

LEVERS AND HANDLES are made with metal rods.

BAMBOO is a naturally occurring tube form. Here, hollow tubes are married with a structure made from solid steel rods to create a chair. Design: Ezri Tarazi for The Nature Conservancy.

THREADING PROVIDES A PRECISE AND REVERSIBLE CONNECTION BETWEEN METAL PARTS.

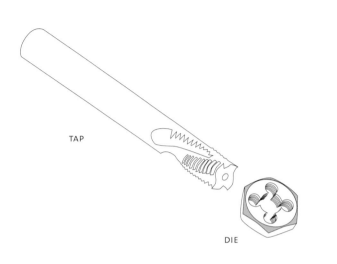

FIX IT. Use special tools to restore an old threaded rod or start a new thread. The tool for creating threads on a bolt is called a die, while that for creating the corresponding thread inside the nut is called a tap. An oil lubricant such as WD-40 spray makes it easy to work with metal and rusted metal parts.

THREADED CONNECTIONS. A cable tension adjuster, a nut and bolt, and a wood clamp are all tools that use threaded rods.

KNURLING is a manufacturing process that cuts or rolls a crisscross pattern onto a metal surface. This texture provides a hand grip. Knurling is generally done on a lathe.

CINCH BENCH is designed for small spaces and lifestyles on the go. The integrated clamp system invites assembly and disassembly, and there is no hardware to lose. Design: Betsy Barnhart.

A tree branch or tree trunk is a rod that naturally occurs in nature. The direction of the fibers runs along the length of the limb, which can bend under force. This same principle is at work in rods milled from wood, which use the direction of the grain to yield a uniform structural material with excellent strength in compression.

Most wooden rods are turned on a lathe. While a rod has a round profile, linear wooden objects such as slats or square-profile dowels have similar properties. Examples of wooden rods include beams, poles, dowels, pencils, and toothpicks. Designers can quickly prototype many kinds of structure using these readily available materials.

DOWEL PLUGS are used to join pieces of wooden furniture. The grooves allow a good fit and a strong glue joint.

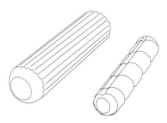

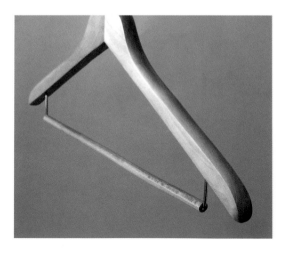

WOODEN HANGERS for clothes use a smooth, varnished dowel to hang trousers. The side-pin assembly allows the rod to rotate for easy use.

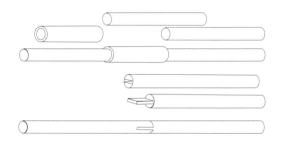

MECHANICAL CONNECTIONS. Even though wood is easy to glue, an additional mechanical connection (such as inserting a rod into an opening) yields a more permanent connection. Using a tube connector is one way to create a strong pole. Using a pin or slot is another solution, but inserting the pin can weaken the wood. When gluing wooden dowels, apply glue not only on the tip but also on the sides of the hinge. Because of the direction of wood fibers, the cross section will suck up a lot of glue, weakening the bond.

MANY EXAMPLES OF WOODEN FURNITURE USE LATHE-TURNED PARTS, INCLUDING TABLE LEGS, NEWEL POSTS, AND CRIB RAILS.

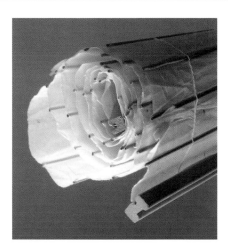

THIN AND LIGHT. Combined with rice paper, wooden rods are used to create this light, strong window shade.

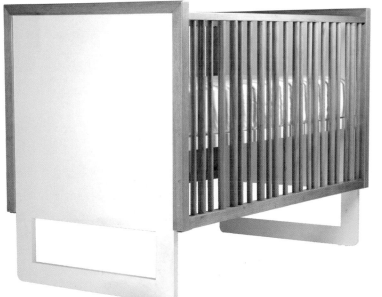

THE ROCKABLE is a surprising stool made of lathed wooden staves with flared, flattened ends. Design: Hans Sandgren Jakobsen.

NURSERYWORKS CRIB uses round wooden rods as a structural as well as decorative element. Design: Nurseryworks.

A tube or pipe is a hollow cylinder for conveying fluid, gas, and other materials, such as wires, in an electrical installation. Tubes can be specified according to standard sizes (such as Nominal Pipe Size in the United States) or according to the material's outside dimension, inside dimensions, and wall thickness. A tube can be rigid or flexible, and it can have a profile that is round, square, or multisided. Tubes, which appear throughout the natural and built world, have many structural uses in addition to providing a means of passage. Material rolled into a tube has greater strength than the same material laid flat, yet it remains lightweight.

BICYCLE FORK. A bicycle structure uses the strength and low minimal weight of tubes. This photo was taken at a shop that recycles old bikes.

BAMBOO POLES become functional furniture. The Nature Conservancy commissioned Ezri Tarazi to design new objects made from bamboo. His designs exploit the hollow structure of large-scale lengths of bamboo. The empty spaces house lighting, speakers, and other components.

A VARIETY OF CUTTING, BENDING, AND CONNECTING TECHNIQUES MAKE IT FUN TO WORK WITH TUBES. SOME DESIGNERS USE STANDARD FITTINGS, WHILE OTHERS USE WELDING.

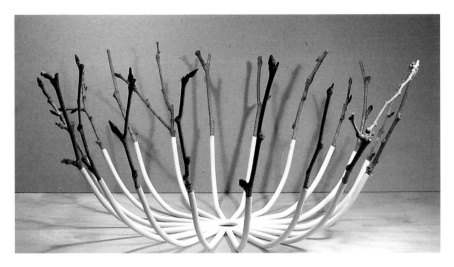

SYCAMORE BOWL from The New Organic design collection contrasts warm, organic twigs with a uniform steel structure. Design and photo: Stanley Ruiz.

BREAK VASE is made from a cut steel tube. Design: skogstad/vold.

PROTOTYPING TECHNIQUES

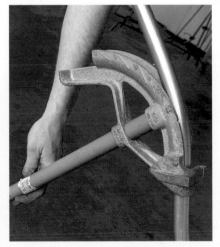

ROOTS. This prototype uses a Y-shaped coupling and poly tube. The device, inspired by plant roots, collects water that would otherwise run off of impermeable surfaces and distribute it to a garden. Design: Inna Alesina.

CONDUIT BENDING TOOL is an easy way to shape metal tubes, including steel pipes.

PVC CONNECTORS make turning corners easy. The designer connected the structures with PVC solvent cement, available in any hardware store. Design: Whitney Wright, MICA.

A hose is a portable, flexible tube. It is typically reinforced with a braided textile to help it withstand pressure from air or liquid.

CLEAR PVC HOSE reveals the flow of liquid inside. The braided reinforcement allows for a higher working pressure.

COILED HOSE saves space. Similarly, your small intestine is coiled inside your body, allowing a long passageway to fit in a minimal space.

FLEXIBLE SURFACE. Vinyl tubing is used as a surface for inexpensive outdoor furniture. Tubes are wrapped around a frame and welded together to stay in place.

SOAP PUMP is a common use of flexible tubing. Design: Method Products.

A BOA CONSTRICTOR CAN STRETCH AROUND SHAPES OR FLEX AS NEEDED.
SIMILARLY, DESIGNERS USE FLEXIBLE TUBES TO MAKE ORGANIC SHAPES.

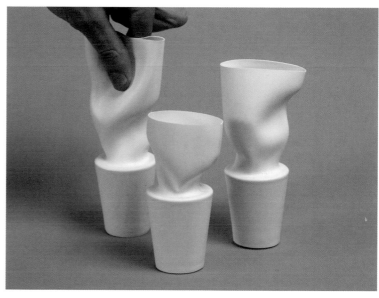

MUTANT VASE. This vase consists of a Slinky (machined from a solid metal tube) held between the top and bottom of a narrower aluminum vase. Design: Giovanni Pellone for Benza.

SKIN SERIES VASES are made from industrial heat-shrink tubing, a plastic material that gets smaller when exposed to intense heat, losing half its size. Design: The Mighty Bearcats (Jason T. Chernak, Steve Haulenbeek, and Bryan Metzdorf). Photo: Keith Evans and Lindsay Williams.

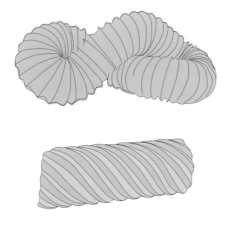

STRUCTURE AND FLEXIBILITY. While the corrugated tube (top) is flexible, diagonal corrugations (bottom) make the tube rigid and structural.

ROCK CANDY. Vinyl tubing was handwoven to create this pouf. Design: Helene Ige.

Spiral-wound tubes are used for packaging, for cores for toilet paper and masking tape, and as forms for poured concrete pillars. Paper tubes are made from fiberboard, paperboard, kraft paper, and composite materials. Unlike metal or plastic, paper tubes do not promote condensation on parts. This inexpensive material is tough and flexible, and made from a renewable, recyclable resource. Spiral-wound forms appear in nature, where structure is created from minimal material. Examples include snail and conch shells. Overlapping spirals of flat material make such structures very strong. We tried bending a rolled tube and a spiral wound carpeting core to see which one was stronger. The rolled tube got easily kinked, while the spiral tube did not.

SONOTUBE is designed to be filled with liquid concrete and then peeled away to reveal a column.

PAPER ARCHITECTURE. Shigeru Ban designed a pavilion for the Singapore Biennale made almost entirely out of recycled paper tubes. Photo: Tom De Gay.

PROTOTYPING TECHNIQUES

LASER CUTTERS, BAND SAWS, AND HAND-CUTTING TOOLS ARE EASY TO USE WITH CARDBOARD TUBES.

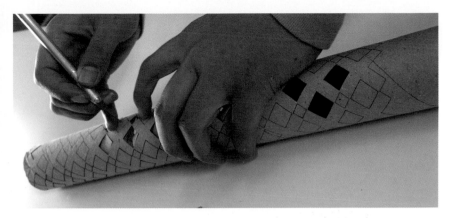

2D TO 3D. The rotary function of a laser cutter allows designers to cut and engrave a cylindrical surface. A flat drawing was wrapped around and cut into the surface of a tube as the rotational arm moved the tube. In the prototype shown here, some parts did not get cut all the way through and needed a little help from an X-Acto knife.

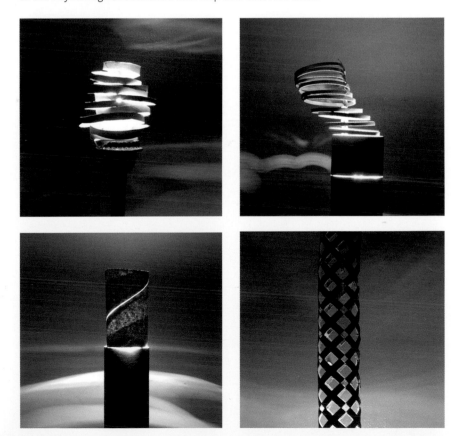

LIGHT STUDIES. These lighting prototypes were created with laser-cut shipping tubes and toilet paper rolls. Design: Hyeshin Kim and Jessica White, MICA.

ROPE/CABLE/YARN

Rope, a length of fibers or yarns that have been twisted or braided together, has tensile strength but not compressive strength; thus it can be used for pulling but not for pushing. Rope can be made from natural fibers such as hemp, linen, cotton, jute, and sisal as well as from metal fibers and from synthetics including polypropylene, nylon, polyester, and polyethylene. Rope is used in construction, exploration, sports, communications, and more. A rich tradition of knot-tying has evolved for making connections that are both beautiful and functional. Cables and ropes are also connected via weaving and a variety of hardware devices. This diverse and ubiquitous material holds endless possibilities for designers. It is easy to work with using readily available studio tools.

CABLE BRIDGE. Tension structures are strong and light.

TENSION ROPE DRUM. Ropes for pulling high-wattage conductor cables are made from strong nylon.

PLAYGROUND EQUIPMENT. This structure is made from ropes and clever connectors.

EXPERIMENT WITH STRING, ROPE, CABLE, YARN, CORD, FISHING WIRE, AND FIBER OPTIC
CABLES. DESIGNERS USE CABLES TO CREATE TENSION STRUCTURES, TO SUSPEND OBJECTS,
AND TO KNIT, KNOT, AND WEAVE STRUCTURES.

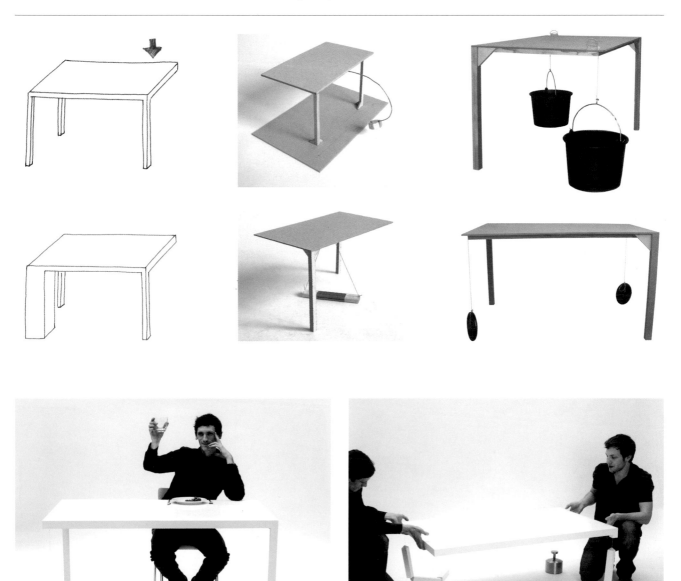

SUPPENKASPAR. A two-legged table looks like it will fall over. This design upsets the user's assumptions and creates an uneasy experience. Although the table can be used as a dining or work surface, the user will always feel its torsion and elasticity. (Sitting on the edge is not advised.) In place of the missing legs are weights connected to thin cables. The designers experimented with various weights and configurations; their most extreme version has legs that are cut into three lengths and held together by tension. Design: Nina Farsen and Isabel Schöllhammer. Photo: Andreas Velten.

Yarn is a component of rope. It is a long, continuous length of interlocked fibers, suitable for use in sewing, crocheting, knitting, weaving, and embroidery. Yarn can be spun in a single cohesive fiber (as in silk), or it can consist of multiple filaments twisted together (as in knitting wool). Textured yarns have characteristics of both spun and filament yarns.

SOFT ELECTRIC TEXTILES. The ElectroPUFF Lamp Dimmer is a pom-pom designed to control an incandescent table lamp; tapping the pom-pom dims the lamp. It is made from a combination of recycled carpet fibers and touch-sensitive conductive yarns. Available as a kit, kids can put the object together as a learning project. Design and photos: Maggie Orth with International Fashion Machines (IFM).

MINIMAL LAMP. The cotton-covered power cords that deliver electricity to these lamps also form their shades; the cords have been hand-crocheted to create colorful webbed forms around the bulbs. Design: Jed Crystal.

PROTOTYPING TECHNIQUES

YARN CAN BE KNITTED, WOVEN, KNOTTED, AND USED TO CONSTRUCT COMPOSITE MATERIALS.

YARN AND GLUE. This balloon wrapped in ball of yarn and glue uses the same technique as the Random Light by Bertjan Pot for Moooi. Pot's design began as a modernist craft project of sorts. After attempts at knitting fiberglass as a way to create structure, Pot turned to coiling epoxy-dipped fiberglass around a large balloon in varying patterns. Once the balloon was popped, the dramatic globe shape remained. Constructed by Inna Alesina.

WARP+WEFT. In this project, optic fiber, TV cable, and electrical cords have been woven into a fabric made from ordinary clothespins. According to the designers, the project addresses society's need for a continuous connection to power and communication lines. The fabric can warp into various forms, acting as a floor, wall, or ceiling. Design: Animish Kudalkar, Steve Vebber, Nathan Van Zuidam, Dave Garbarz, Krishna Kanth Samavedam, In Jin Cha, and Parker Brock, University of Illinois at Urbana-Champaign.

RUBBER

Rubber is a sensual material with numerous functional characteristics. It can be used as a coating and molded into shapes. It comes in sheets (floor mats) and strands (inside a bungee cord). It is dip-molded to create condoms, balloons, and rubber gloves. It can be sealed and filled with air or water. It bounces, stretches, and protects. It can be stitched, glued, and cut. Natural rubber (latex) is harvested from the rubber tree and stabilized with sulphur and an accelerating process called vulcanizing. Synthetic rubber is made from a variety of polymer materials.

Rubber is used as a grip on bike handles, kitchen tools, and toothbrushes. There are many common sources of rubber for use in making prototypes. Repurpose rubber bands, bike inner tubes, or rubber sheets, or use liquid rubber for dipping and fastening objects together.

HUGE SUCTION CUP. This special holder used for carrying plate glass uses the principle of the suction cup. Rubber is flexible, and when it is pulled away from the surface, it creates a vacuum and grips the glass safely.

SILICONE RUBBER KITCHEN FUNNEL has a collapsible shape inspired by an old camera, whose soft sunscreen folded out like an accordion and folded away when not in use. Design: Boje Estermann for Normann Copenhagen. Photo: Normann Copenhagen.

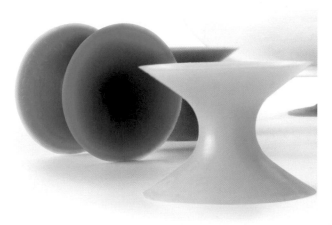

NAPFNAPF is a double-sided silicone suction cup used to connect a plate to any smooth table to help prevent table spills. Design: Beat Karrer. Photo: Luca Zanier.

RUBBER CAN BE MOLDED INTO ENDLESS SHAPES AND TEXTURES.

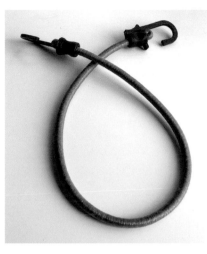

TIRES are a common use of rubber. The treads and inner tube use several properties of the material, including its grip, softness, resilience, and airtightness.

BUNGEE CORD. Threads of rubber encased in a braided sleeve become multipurpose fasteners. The braiding regulates how much the rubber can stretch, making the bungee cord a long-lasting object. Bungee cords combined into mesh structures are used as cargo nets for cars.

OXO GOOD GRIPS. A famous example of universal design, this vegetable peeler features a Santoprene rubber grip grooved with flexible ridges. The product's thickness, texture, and weight make it feel good in the hand. Design: Smart Design.

SQUEEGEES are used in the silk screen process to push ink through the tight mesh of the screen. The flexibility of the rubber makes it the perfect material for this tool.

DOORMAT. A carpet base with a "printed" or molded rubber overlay makes an inexpensive, functional, and visually intriguing solution for a doormat.

SILICONE RUBBER is heat resistant, hygienic, food safe, and easy to clean. It is used in many kitchen gadgets, from oven gloves to baking pans. Design: Orka.

COVERED OBJECT FRAME. Put any object under the rubber skin to create wall art. Design and photo: Martin Konrad Gloeckle.

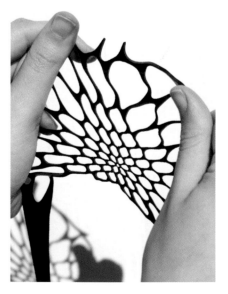

INNER TUBES salvaged from bicycles can be cut and stitched into useful objects. Industrial markings and irregularities make the objects more interesting. Design: Inna Alesina.

INNER TUBE LAMP consists of rubber stretched around a tubular glass bulb. The shade takes its shape from the bulb. Design and photo: Sylvain Willenz Design Studio.

RADIOLARIA JEWELRY is made from sheets of silicone rubber cut with a pattern of ellipses. The flexible silicone wraps around the body. Design: Jesse Louis-Rosenberg and Jessica Rosenkrantz, Nervous System.

OBJECTS CAN BE DIPPED INTO RUBBER IN ITS LIQUID FORM. LIQUID RUBBER CAN ALSO BE USED TO PRINT GRIP PATTERNS ONTO FABRIC AND OTHER SURFACES.

DR. BAMBOOZLE. Lengths of bamboo were strapped together and dipped in yellow rubber. The cured rubber bonds the bamboo together to create simple stools. Design: James Carrigan and Sylvain Willenz. Photo: Sylvain Willenz Design Studio.

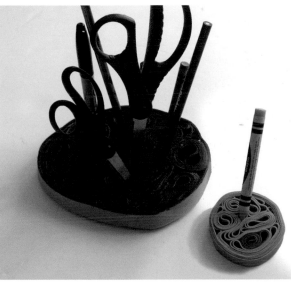

DESKTOP CADDY made from large rubber bands dipped in rubber. The coating serves both as decoration and as fastener. Design: Alexandra Zahn and Marnay Harris, MICA.

SHEET METAL

Sheet metal is used in many objects, from soda cans and aluminum foil to airplane wings. Most metals are available in sheet form, from delicate membranes such as gold leaf to thick slabs of steel or aluminum. Measured in gages, sheet metal is easily shaped, perforated, cut, and stamped. Besides being rolled, sheet metal can be made by spinning, a process that leaves characteristic lines on the surface and allows for the manufacture of a precise wall thickness, as in a cymbal instrument. Industrial techniques include etching, die-cutting, jet cutting, and computer numerical controlled (CNC) cutting. Finishes, including printing, galvanizing, anodizing, polishing, brushing, powder coating, and chromium coating, can be protective, decorative, or both.

The kitchen is a place to find all kinds of sheet metal in use. Look at flatware, jar lids, pots, and the spout on a box of dishwasher detergent as well as the oven, refrigerator, and microwave.

Pure metals are easily recycled, while alloys can only be down-cycled (used to create less valuable products). For example, a soda can uses three different kinds of aluminum alloy, so it cannot be made into new cans, which require pure materials.

SEVERAL ALUMINUM ALLOYS are used in a typical soda can, which also employs a variety of joining techniques. The top of the can is rolled to the sides, and the pull tab is riveted.

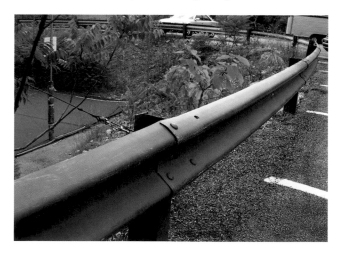

CORRUGATED EDGE RAIL is made structurally strong by the bends in the material. The nesting, overlapping ends are riveted together.

PERFORATION reduces the amount of material and allows light and substances to pass through the surface.

BENDING AND SHAPING A SHEET OF METAL PRODUCES A STRUCTURAL VOLUME.

CUTOUTS of this trashcan are bent to create a bottom. Design: Dan Gioia, MICA.

THINOLOGY. A sheet of laser-cut steel is shaped by hand to form a 3D object. The resulting plane "remembers" its flat origin. Design: Ronen Kadushin.

INFLATABLE STEEL. Suitable for growing plants indoors or outdoors, these planters look like inflated structures. The planters can hold soil, pots, or water for pond plants. Design: Stephen Newby.

BOTTLE CAPS are crimped to create an air-tight connection. Crimping metal creates connections without using bolts or screws.

AIRPLANE WINGS use riveting as a fastening technique. Rivets provide a mechanical connection that is much stronger than welding (a chemical connection).

SCISSORS are the icon for cutting, and they themselves are cut out of a flat sheet of steel. Did you know you can sharpen scissors with aluminum foil?

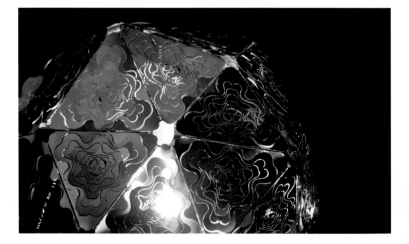

JANTRA LIGHT from Renue Series is made from laser-cut facets of stainless steel sheets. Design: Suppapong Sonsang. Photo: Natthadist Atitcharoenphong.

PROTOTYPING TECHNIQUES

USE EVERYDAY MATERIALS TO MAKE PROTOTYPES OF METAL OBJECTS.

CUT AND FOLD a soda can to make new forms and objects.

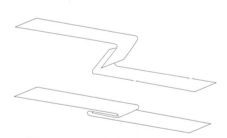

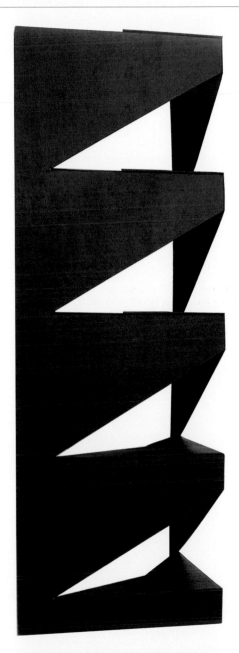

ALUMINUM FLASHING is available in rolled sheets and is easy to work with. Cut it with scissors or punch it with a sharp object like a nail. Bend and fold to create connections.

PROTOTYPE FOR A METAL BOOKSHELF is made with illustration board. It was sprayed with paint to simulate a powder-coated finish. Design: Kimberly Ruppert, MICA.

Stainless steel resists stains, corrosion, and rust. It is a steel alloy that contains at least 11 percent chromium by mass. The chromium generates a protective film that deters degradation of the material. Stainless steel is the material of choice for many designers when durability and clean looks are important. It also has spring metal properties and thus is commonly used for clips and other objects where the memory of metal is important.

SELF-RETRACTING TAPE MEASURE employs a curved metallic ribbon that remains stiff and straight when extended, but retracts into a coil for convenient storage.

FLAT SPRING PARTS are commonly used in clips.

LAMP SHADE consists of a single sheet of metal that has been slit to create both shade and attachment. Design and photo: Sebastian Bergne.

MATERIALS WITH MEMORY ARE USED BY DESIGNERS TO CREATE
RESPONSIVE TEXTILES, SWITCHES, AND LIGHT FIXTURES.

Bimetals, composed of two metals with different properties, change in response to rising or falling temperatures. This principle has been used in various devices since the eighteenth century. Today, such thermally reactive metals are at work in numerous household electronics. Some thermostats contain a coiled strip of bimetal that tightens and triggers a switch when temperatures drop, turning on a furnace or heater.

RESPONSIVE LIGHT FIXTURE. The elements of this pendant lamp, called Protea, move away from heat. When the light is off, the shade is cool and closes around the bulb like an unopened blossom. When the lamp is turned on and generates heat, the petals spread away from the bulb. The aluminum ring at the top of the lamp wraps around the petals and holds them together. Design: Karl Zahn.

TRUSS

A truss uses triangular elements to span, reinforce, or support walls, ceilings, or beams. In a plane truss, all elements lie within a 2D plane. In a space truss, elements extend into three dimensions. A truss can be built with tiny toothpicks or huge steel beams. Trusses are the basis of structures that can bear large loads with a minimum of materials.

STEEL LATTICE is a widespread structure for power towers and other tall structures. It provides tremendous strength and resistance to wind while making minimal use of materials. Consider how little material the steel lattice uses as compared with a solid tree trunk.

TRUSS BRIDGE is a common construction.

MANY EVERYDAY OBJECTS USE SMART STRUCTURAL ELEMENTS. DESIGNERS OFTEN USE READY-MADE COMPONENTS TO CREATE PROTOTYPES OR INSTALLATIONS.

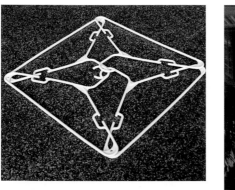

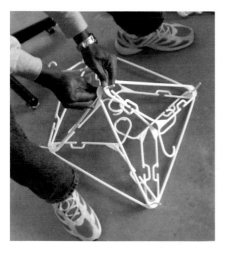

MUNDANE[UPGRADE]. Students in a design/fabricate seminar created a building block module out of plastic hangers. They used zip ties to lash the modules together. The lacy, transparent, yet surprisingly strong structure is similar to large-scale spaceframe constructions that employ steel trusses. Design: Sam Bowen, Ka Kit, David Ho, Blake Knapp, Ben Loeffler, Charlie Lutz, and Darren Glisan, University of Illinois at Urbana-Champaign, School of Architecture.

WEBBING/STRAP

Webbing is a strong strip or tube of woven fabric that often serves as a strap or connector. It is a functional component in the design of furniture, safety equipment, parachuting, military apparel, fire hoses, and many other applications. It can be made from high-strength materials such as nylon, polyester, and Kevlar as well as from natural fibers such as cotton and flax. The remarkable strength of webbing has long been exploited in seat belts and other safety devices. Nylon webbing is used extensively in rock climbing, where its high strength and light weight make it the ideal material for slings, runners, harnesses, and more.

Low-cost, high-strength plastic webbing can be used to hold together stacks of newspapers or magazines, to secure large packages, and to attach large loads to shipping crates. Straps can be connected via heat fusing or by crimping with a special tool. This ubiquitous utilitarian material has many uses for designers.

SEAT BELTS must be lightweight and comfortable yet capable of withstanding tremendous force during an accident. The wide, flat material prevents injury; a thin rope could cut into a person.

FOOTWEAR STRAPS. Durable, nonstretch, easily sewn, and available in many colors, webbing is an attractive choice for sports shoes and backpacks. Adjustable clasps, hook and loop fasteners, and other hardware work well with webbing. Design and photo: Keen.

WOVEN. This bag is woven from colorful reclaimed industrial strapping.

USE WEBBING AS A TENSION SUPPORT, CARRYING STRAP, OR A REINFORCEMENT FOR SPORTS PRODUCTS. CLASPS, SIDE RELEASE BUCKLES, VELCRO, D-RINGS, AND OTHER HARDWARE ARE USED WITH WEBBING STRAPS.

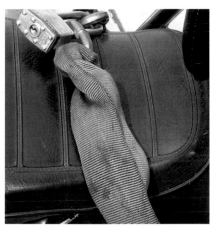

WEBBED COVER for a bike chain protects the bike finish from the metal chain inside. The additional material also makes it harder for a thief to cut through the chain, because different tools are needed to cut each material.

TUBULAR WEBBING is used for this water hose. The tube flattens when not in use, saving space compared with round tubing of the same length and capacity.

TENSION SUPPORT. The Crazy Creek chair uses the tension and counterweight of the user's legs to support the back during sitting. Webbing straps give the chair its primary structure. Photo courtesy of Crazy Creek.

CARPET SEAT. This round rug splits into two parts; each part can be folded to create a seat. Webbing is integrated into the design to create nonstretch sides. The user's weight locks the seat open, and the tension of the webbing creates back support. Design: Inna Alesina. Photo: Gleb Kutepov.

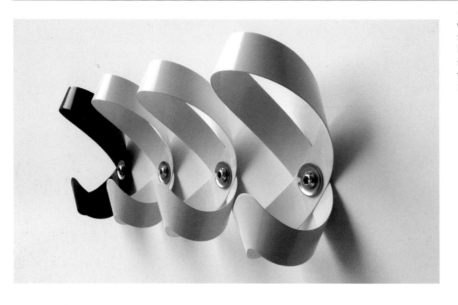

COAT HOOK Flat strips of stainless spring steel become strong hooks when they are looped into figure-8s. The pieces fold flat for shipping; the user mounts them to the wall with a standard screw and washer. Design: Nicola Enrico Stäubli. Photo: Rolf Küng.

STRAP CHAIR employs straps traditionally used in shipping and packing. Wrapped around a chair frame, the straps provide both surface and structure. They are connected with an industrial crimper and metal clips. Design: Constantin Boym and Laurene Leon Boym.

PROTOTYPING TECHNIQUES

WEBBING CAN BE SEWN, WOVEN, CRIMPED, RIVETED, AND CLASPED. TENSIONERS AND CRIMPERS ARE TOOLS USED TO CREATE PERMANENT CONNECTIONS BETWEEN WEBBED ELEMENTS.

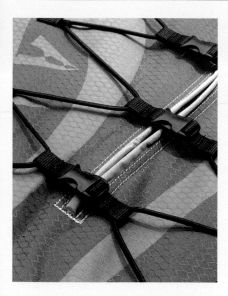

CONNECTIONS. Designers use all kinds of webbing connections, from huge parachute clasps and D-rings to multifunctional straps incorporating safety whistles, LED lights, and compasses.

CRIMPING TOOL and steel crimps are used for fastening together webbing and straps.

DOMESTIC CLAMPS create nonpermanent joints, allowing users to assemble their own structures from available materials. Webbing can connect all kinds of shapes together, including round to round. Design: David Schafer and Im Schafer for Studiomake. Photo: Travis Roozee.

TIP: A packaging supplies catalog is a good place to find all kinds of strapping connectors, tensioning tools, and crimps.

PLASTIC STRAPS FROM PACKAGING. These colorful straps were reclaimed from grocery stores, where they are used to secure boxes. Stores use color-coded straps to communicate the type of product contained inside. The straps can be melted and fused on a foil-covered frying pan. A coil form is an easy way to sculpt shapes from strapping.

WIRE

A wire is a long strand of drawn metal, usually cylindrical in section. It can be flexible or rigid, thick or thin. Aluminum, copper, nickel, and steel wires carry electricity and telecommunications signals and conduct heat. Wire is also used to build load-bearing structures and surfaces. It is a basic component in other important materials, including netting, fabric, and rope. Wire is used to build fences, cages, and suspension bridges. It is also a defining element of numerous stringed musical instruments.

This beautiful material is easy to experiment with. Everyday wire fasteners include everything from nails and straight pins to staples and twist ties. A wire's gauge is its diameter or cross section. The gauge determines how much electrical current the material can safely carry as well as its electrical resistance and its weight per unit of length.

SMOOTH FINISH. Wire baskets and shopping carts are usually powder coated or plated to withstand the elements. Other finishes include galvanizing and anodizing.

METAL FABRIC. Stainless steel wire curtains are used for architectural dividers. They are durable and allow air and light to pass through.

STAINLESS STEEL WHISK is used for beating eggs and mixing cake batter. The multiple wires loop are designed to quickly beat air into mixtures.

WIRE IS A VERSATILE MATERIAL THAT CAN BE AS TOUGH AS NAILS OR SOFT AS SILK. DESIGNERS USE WIRE TO CREATE STRUCTURAL ARMATURES AND TRANSPARENT OR FLEXIBLE SURFACES.

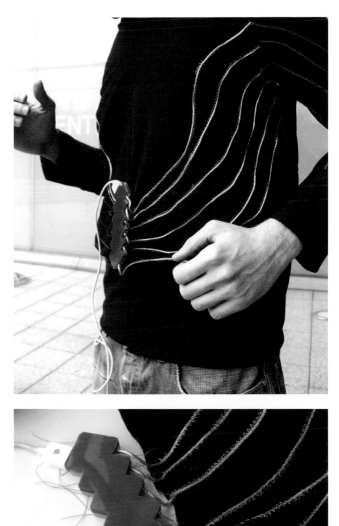

FLEXIBLE CONCRETE. The seat of this chair is made of linked concrete blocks. Each block was cast with wire "ears." After the concrete cured, the blocks were connected with wires to create a comfortable seat suspended on a steel frame. Design: Kwok Pan Fung, MICA.

POWER JACKET uses a person's movements and the friction between layers of fabric and body parts to generate electricity. Wires both conduct electrical current to the charging device and create a ribbed texture for maximum energy generation. Concept design: Madeline Peters, MICA.

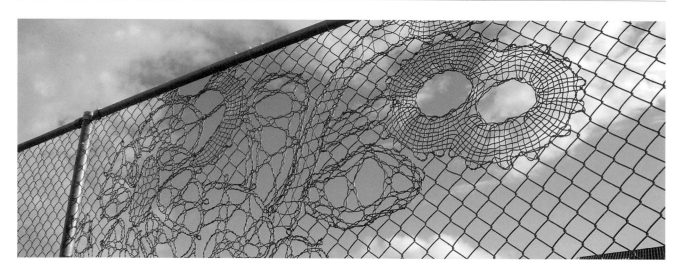

LACE FENCE. This fence is made from both wire and chain link. Craft meets industry as a segment of factory-made material becomes a lyrical ornament. Design: Demakersvan / Jeroen Verhoeven, Joep Verhoeven, and Judith de Graauw. Photo: Raoul Kramer.

STEEL-WIRE SIDE TABLE also functions as a tray, bowl, and trash can. Design: Stephen Burks for Artecnica.

HANGING FIXTURE. This graceful hanging lantern is made from recycled wire coat hangers. Design: 101.

WIRE IS A STRONG BUT FLEXIBLE MATERIAL. LIKE A FIBER, IT CAN BE WOVEN, STITCHED, KNOTTED, AND BRAIDED.

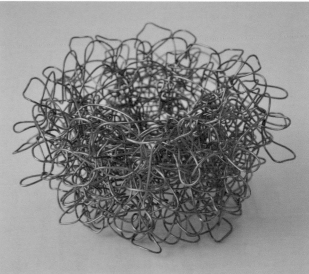

CROCHET CROCHET. The designer used crochet stitches to transform 3,000 feet of aluminum wire into a woven structure that can bear considerable weight. Although the piece resembles at first glance a casual tangle of wire, it actually follows a careful construction process. The 3D sphere took shape as the designer progressed from smaller to larger gauges of wire. Anodizing the finished piece added stability. Design: Ruth Fore, RISD.

Wire springs are used in a wide variety of products, from mattresses to paper clips. The harder the wire, the stronger the spring.

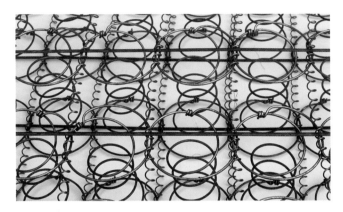

BEDSPRINGS support our bodies at rest. The large surface of a bed must provide different support at different pressure points. Bedsprings achieve this with minimal material use. This elegant everyday object is usually hidden from our eyes.

FLEXIBLE DRYER HOSE uses a coiled spring-wire structure. The skin is usually made of vinyl or aluminum.

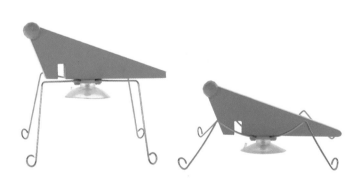

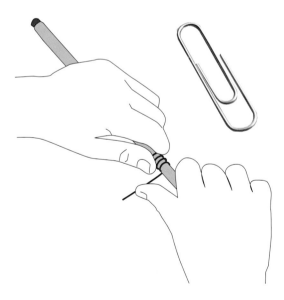

LEOPOLD. A steel spring gives this jumping critter toy its charming, lifelike behavior. Design: Chico Bicalho for Kikkerland.

EVERYDAY SPRING. A paperclip is essentially a spring. The memory of the wire serves to clip the paper together. For building prototypes, you can fashion a simple spring from a paper clip by wrapping the wire around a pencil or other cylinder. Use pliers to bend harder wire.

DESIGNERS USE SPRING WIRE TO CREATE MINIMAL STRUCTURES. ENERGY IS STORED IN THE SPRING, ALLOWING DESIGNERS TO CREATE OBJECTS THAT WOULD OTHERWISE REQUIRE MORE MATERIAL TO PERFORM A SIMILAR FUNCTION.

WIRE WIT. Heavy Guy lamp uses a thin, bouncy wire to mount a fixture to the wall. Design: Mischa Vos, Ontwerp Studio.

CONTINUOUS TITANIUM WIRE is the basis of this ingenious eyewear. The lenses are cut with a reverse groove so that the wire nests inside the perimeter of the lens. A continuous length of wire surrounds the lenses and forms the nose bridge. This design uses minimal soldering and few moving parts, yielding a durable product. Beta titanium wire is used for its light weight and flexibility. Design: Alan Tipp.

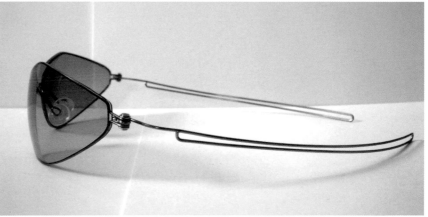

WOOD

Wood is one of the world's most commonly used materials. It has been employed for millennia to make furniture, tools, weapons, buildings, boats, and works of art. Wood is a renewable, reusable, and biodegradable resource. If it is harvested wisely, it can be used to benefit human society without destroying forests. The Forest Stewardship Council certifies wood that has been responsibly harvested around the world for use in making construction materials as well as paper.

CRATING. Pine wood planks are commonly used for shipping. Wooden palettes make up a substantial portion of landfills.

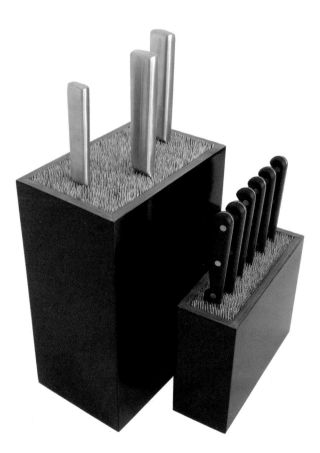

MIKOTO is a wooden frame filled with hundreds of bamboo skewers that support cooking knives and other tools without damaging blades or requiring custom-made slots. Design: Martin Robitsch. Photo: Boo Louis for Ekobo.

ROOF SHINGLES. Most wood-shingled roofs are made from western red cedar. Wood shingles provide air circulation and weather resistance.

PROTOTYPING TECHNIQUES

BENT WOOD PROVIDES A LIGHT STRUCTURE FOR FURNITURE. IT IS A COMPLICATED PROCESS BUT POSSIBLE TO IMPLEMENT IN A SHOP.

JIG for bending wood for a snowshoe. Pieces of hardwood are softened in a steamer and clamped in place to set in the desired shape.

STEAMER softens the wood. A kettle of boiling water produces constant steam for use inside a closed wooden box. The designer checks the temperature inside the box and adds boiling water from an electric kettle to create more steam.

RESTORING OLD FURNITURE is a good way to learn about furniture construction methods. Old wooden chairs use quality bent wood pieces that can be easily reclaimed.

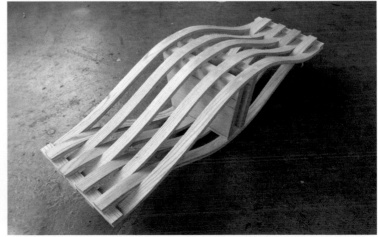

WOVEN WOOD. Cutting wood or bamboo into thin strips that can be coiled or woven into 3D shapes is an ancient technique. Here, hardwood was sawed into thin ribbons and glued around a jig to create a rocking stool. Design: Antoine Heath, MICA.

Plywood is a composite, engineered material made from thin sheets of veneer that are peeled away from a tree log. Plywood manufacturing, unlike the milling of planks, conserves materials because the peeling process produces no sawdust waste or unusable half-rounds at the outside of the log. The veneers or plies are glued together in layers whose grains are laid at opposing angles. (In bendable plywood, all the grains run in one direction.) Heat, pressure, and strong adhesives bond the plies together. The large, flat sheets of material are convenient and economical. Veneer is also used to make musical instruments, including guitars and violins, and for making bent wood.

Bamboo, which can be made into veneers and plywood, is a nontimber renewable resource used around the world for everything from food and shelter to fuel and fabric. Its tensile strength is superior to that of steel.

BAMBU PLATE, an alternative to paper dishes, is made by molding bamboo veneers into shapes. Design: Bambu.

ENORMOUS ARMCHAIR is made from reclaimed shipping crates that still have stamps and painted logos on the surface. Design: Piet Hein Eek. Photograph: Nob Ruijgrok.

BENT WOOD, PLYWOOD, AND VENEER ALL START AS THIN FLEXIBLE SHEETS. DESIGNERS MANIPULATE THE PROPERTIES OF THE MATERIAL TO ACHIEVE A DESIRED RESULT. IN THE FINAL OBJECT, WOOD VENEER CAN BE EITHER FLEXIBLE OR RIGID.

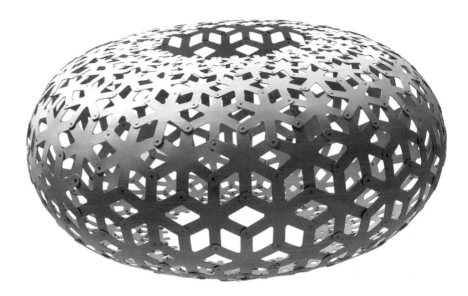

SNOWFLAKE hanging lamp is made of hoop pine plywood and aluminum rivets. The timber comes from sustainably managed plantations. All pieces are designed to use the minimum amount of material for the maximum effect. The product ships in a flat pack for low-energy freighting. Design: David Trubridge.

LOVI is a Finnish company that makes flat-pack holiday decorations that can be sent as holiday greetings. The company used the same technique to create the Pumpkin stool above, made from medium-density fiberboard. Design: Anne Paso.

TONTON STOOL also functions as a magazine holder and table base. The curve provides structural resistance while forming a comfortable seat and an attractive visual profile. The lightweight and portable piece is made from cold-formed plywood finished with veneer and covered with colored lacquer. Design and photo: Patricia Naves.

INTELLECTUAL PROPERTY
Has this been made before? Can I make it without infringing on other people's patents? Can I protect my idea?

MARKET RESEARCH
Who will buy it? What features will users want? How will it look and in what colors? How will it be packaged?

SALES AND DISTRIBUTION
Where will the product be sold? In stores? Online? To specialized or general markets?

MANUFACTURING
What materials will it be made from? Can the product be mass-produced? Where will it be made? Will it be affordable?

MAKE IT REAL

FROM PROTOTYPE TO PRODUCT

The design process starts with a problem. Then comes research and prototyping. Along the way, designers ask a lot of questions. What do users want? What has been done before? What is good for people and the environment? How do materials look, feel, and behave? Finally, when we have developed a strong and vivid concept, we need to go back and do it all again, but on another level. This process is like traveling in a circle that narrows down with each cycle, taking you closer to your goal.

Now that you have identified a problem and created a potential solution, you must confirm your findings again. You will need to find out if your idea can be protected (intellectual property research). You will need to protect your idea as you communicate with potential business partners (nondisclosure agreements). You will need to make clear, unambiguous drawings to get price quotes (specs) and look for manufacturers (sourcing). You will need to look at the market to see where your product could be sold, and you will need to think about how much people would be willing to pay for your product (market research). You will need to calculate the costs for manufacturing, packaging, shipping, and so on to come up with an estimated retail price. You will need to find out if people will want your product (more market research). You will need to get samples, test them, and have other people test them. You will need to take photographs and organize a presentation. You will need to come up with a name, logo, instructions, and packaging and label concepts. You will need to make a business plan.

And after completing the final process of production, sales, and distribution, you might see a stranger using or wearing your design. Then you will know it is real.

REFINE AND DEVELOP

The foam sandal shown here went through many transformations from conceiving the initial idea to producing samples that could be worn and tested. Colors, textures, details, graphics, and the durometer (hardness) of the material all had to be studied during the development phase. Much of the work was done by hand using ordinary studio tools. The final product has a sleek, high-tech appearance, but getting there was a hands-on process. A good product designer must be a skilled sculptor.

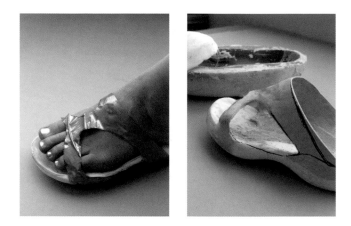

PROTOTYPE. We developed our early concept quickly by combining a plaster foot bed with duct tape uppers. This prototype could not be tested or worn, however, because it was made from a hard material. For the second prototype, we made the upper shape out of metal mesh and refined it with a layer of Bondo, a filler used in auto-body work to fill in dents or creases.

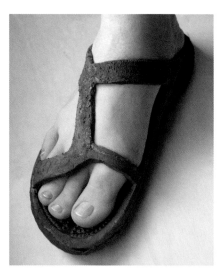

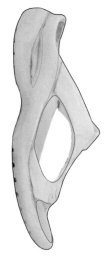

DIVERSE CONDITIONS. We needed to test the treads of the shoe on wet surfaces as well as dry ones. We prototyped and tested a variety of tread designs. We sliced pieces out of a real foam shoe and glued them to get the right materials for testing.

GOT IT. Finally we arrived at the most comfortable, attractive, and functional shape. The completed design feels good on the foot and does not slip off or "flip flop" while walking.

DESIGN SPEC. To communicate the shape of the shoe to the manufacturer, we sent drawings and photographs with notes as well as the physical prototype. The red and blue lines show the desired shape. Design: Inna Alesina.

AFTER ARRIVING AT THE DESIGN WE WANTED, WE WERE READY TO TALK WITH A MANUFACTURER ABOUT POTENTIAL PROBLEMS AND GET A QUOTE ON PRODUCTION COSTS. YOU CAN GET QUOTES FROM BOTH DOMESTIC AND OVERSEAS MANUFACTURERS.

For a list of American manufacturers go to www.thomasnet.com

Do the numbers: Use a volume breakdown to see how your cost will go down if you produce 5,000 objects instead of 500.

PICKING COLORS sounds fun and easy, but in fact it is a difficult decision to make. Consumers want a range of options, but too many choices can be overwhelming.

CHANGES. When the first prototypes arrived from the manufacturer, they were not exactly the right shape, and they had no texture. We communicated changes via photographs and drawings.

TO GET A QUOTE FROM A MANUFACTURER, YOU WILL NEED TO PROVIDE THE FOLLOWING:
- Drawing or sketch with dimensions.
- Specification of desired materials.
- Material samples, if you already know the material you want to use.
- A physical prototype if possible.
- The volume of production.

THE MANUFACTURER'S QUOTE SHOULD ADDRESS THE FOLLOWING:
- Minimums
- Estimated time
- Tooling cost
- Setup cost
- Unit cost
- Material cost
- Freight cost

YOU ALSO MAY REQUEST MATERIALS SPECIFICATION INFORMATION:
- Ask the manufacturer to provide as much information as possible; understand that the manufacturer may have limited data.
- Do your own research about materials, adhesives, and other techniques to make better design decisions.

PROTECT YOUR PROPERTY

Intellectual property (IP) protection is the process of patent search and protection. If you would like to benefit from your design, you will need to make sure of two things: that you are not infringing on someone else's IP, and that you are protecting yourself while you are investigating what to do next. You also need to know whether you are trying to protect the way your invention *looks* or the way it *works*. Design patents protect the way inventions look. Utility patents protect the way they function.

To conduct simple patent research, go to uspto .gov or google.com/patents, and do some general online searches as well. Try different key words and keep your description broad. Do not get discouraged if you see that your invention has already been patented. You may still be able to protect some aspects of it. Your invention will probably change as it develops (functionally and visually), so it may be too early to file a final patent.

A provisional patent is an inexpensive way to protect your invention temporarily. This patent only works if you file a utility patent within one year. A provisional patent will allow you to say "patent pending" on your invention. You do not have to write your claim in legal language; simply describe your invention in a clear, detailed way so that any person with the needed skills could understand and execute your design. It helps to include photographs or drawings. You can file the patent for a reasonable fee. If you later decide to complete a utility patent, the file date will be set to the date you submitted your provisional patent.

Filing a utility or design patent takes more time and expertise, and you will likely need help from a professional patent attorney or patent agent. You might also choose to have a professional patent search done, after you have done your own informal web and patent scouting.

You do not need to have a patent to sell your designs. In developing your product, however, you will be sharing all or part of your idea with other people—you will have to show it to manufacturers for quotes and to potential business partners, banks, retail stores, and customers. A nondisclosure agreement, or NDA, is a commonly used protection. Ask anyone who views your idea to sign an NDA first.

Document your progress and keep signed and dated sketches. Take photos of every model variation you make. These records will help you during the patent process.

COMMON IP MISTAKES
• Do not think that just because you have an idea, you can benefit from it by having someone else implement the idea for a share of the profit. Developing the idea and making it real takes time and effort.
• Do not think your patent attorney will be able to tell you if your ideas will earn you millions. A patent attorney is not a venture capitalist or a business adviser.
• Do not think that simply by patenting your invention you have ensured that it will be produced and become a successful product. Protecting your idea doesn't get it manufactured and sold.
• Do not think that simply by patenting your invention you have ensured that no one will take your idea. IP protection works only if you enforce it.

NONDISCLOSURE AGREEMENT
You can download a sample NDA at www.bitlaw.com/forms/nda.html. An NDA can be a simple, clearly written agreement that states the following:

Inventor such-and-such and business such-and-such would like to tell each other some information and keep it secret. They are doing this for purposes of quoting/ manufacturing/evaluating the secret item, or to decide if they are interested in entering into another arrangement (licensing, selling, etc.), signed and dated by both parties.

DESIGNERS USE PATENTS TO PROTECT THEIR IDEAS.

DESIGN PATENT for foam sandal. The purpose of these drawings is to show the shape of the shoe, since design patents protect only the way inventions look.

Fig. 5

Fig. 6

Fig. 7

UTILITY PATENT for an inflatable pool lounger. The complete patent includes 53 claims and 18 drawings to explain every feature that is protected by the patent. A utility patent addresses the way inventions work. This floating lounger could have a different shape, but the way it works is protected. The patent documents every possible variation or embodiment of the product, such as a strap to connect multiple loungers. Better safe than sorry.

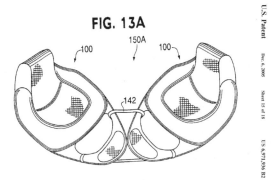

FIG. 13A

MANUFACTURING

You have developed your product and conducted some basic patent searches. You have found that nothing quite like your invention exists. You have some quotes and samples from manufacturers.

You know that your product is possible to make, and you believe that people will buy it. You are looking for a potential venue for it. Here are three paths you might consider.

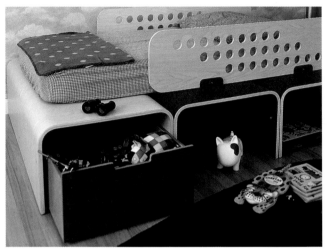

Scenario 1
Make the product in your garage and sell it from your website, on eBay, or at fairs and markets.

PROS. You will have minimal investment, overhead, and risk—just your time and materials. This approach could be your first step to Scenario 2 or 3. You still can outsource some parts to other shops, but you will be responsible for making it all happen. Your process will be easy to manage (no delayed shipments).

CONS. Not everyone has the desire and capability to do self-production. This method works for small volumes only.

Scenario 2
Find someone else to make your product, and you sell it directly via website, catalog, trade shows, etc.

PROS. You are not limited by the capability of your own shop, and you can accommodate larger orders. In fact, you will have to do large orders to get a better manufacturing price.

CONS. You will have shipping and warehousing costs. You will remain responsible for issues such as customer service, order fulfillment, and shipping tracking.

TRUBA is a shelf for charging cell phones and holding keys, ID cards, and other small objects. It can be used as a single unit or arranged into a decorative wall display. It is made from 100% recycled paperboard mailing tubes sourced from a local mill. Shapes are laser-cut and then dyed, hand-finished, and coated with several layers of a protective finish. TRUBA is packaged in a second tube that doubles as a shipper; the hand-stamped graphics indicate places for positioning postage and a shipping label, making it intuitive for customers to reuse the package as a mailing tube. To make sure all processes and materials are green, we chose a local laser cutter and finished the products ourselves, air drying them without using any artificial energy. Design: Inna Alesina.

MODULAR TODDLER BED by Paza Design was developed by Pazit Kagel, a designer who is the mother of three children. This crib can change as the kids grow. The bentwood pieces cannot fold for shipping, so Kagel decided to produce the unit in North America. After getting price quotes, she ordered samples and took them to the International Contemporary Furniture Fair (ICFF) in New York City and began selling to retailers. It was a learning experience. Pieces never arrived on time, and prices kept changing with each order. However, Kagel persevered and expanded her collection. Today, she owns Modern Mini, a successful online store for kids. She has also opened a physical showroom. As she designs more furniture, she will already have an outlet for her pieces and will be able to make design decisions based on her retail experience.

IF YOU WANT TO LICENSE YOUR IDEA, LEARN ABOUT MANUFACTURERS AND BRANDS WITH WHOM YOU WOULD LIKE TO WORK. EACH COMPANY HAS A SPECIAL DEPARTMENT THAT DEALS WITH OUTSIDE INVENTORS. SOME COMPANIES WON'T EVEN LOOK AT IDEAS THAT ARE NOT PATENTED. DO YOUR RESEARCH BEFORE MAKING CONTACT.

PRODUCTION FACILITIES for making molded foam shoes in China. Photo: Harry Abramson.

ARUBA women's sandal by Waldies; final product made in the factory.

Scenario 3
Find a company that is already selling products in your category and try to license your idea to it.

PROS. This is a good scenario for designers who want to focus on design rather than on business issues. You can be compensated for your work with a design fee, a royalty, or both.

CONS. It is hard work to find a company to license your invention. A given company may already have designers working on a similar product, or perhaps your idea won't fit into their line or their current business plan. You'll need luck and connections to succeed.

WALDIES INC. has a reputation for making comfortable foam clogs for kayakers and was looking to expand their line of shoes. We approached this company and struck an agreement: we will design a line of shoes and if the company likes the designs, they will license them. We developed a super comfortable lady's sandal, and the company licensed the design. It was a good scenario because the company provided feedback and took part in the development. Even though it was a licensing agreement, in reality it was a close collaboration. It would be nearly impossible to do a self-production or limited-run of molded shoes. This product requires mass production, and the tooling cost is expensive. Also, it would be hard to sell just one style of shoes without the brand to support you.

Other ways to get started: submit your ideas to design competitions and see what happens.

COMMUNICATE AND PRESENT

Regardless of how you choose to produce your ideas, you will need to explain your work to different people, including employers, investors, clients, retailers, consumers, and the press. Be sure to document your progress along the way. Every designer should learn how to take good pictures of their products and organize them for use in compelling presentations.

Promotional Images

Consider these issues when creating images for press, marketing, and other public uses.

Create high-resolution images, at least 300 dpi.

Take both horizontal and vertical shots. Shoot details as well as overall views.

To tell a story, take pictures of your product in use.

Shots of your object silhouetted against a white background will be preferred by many magazines and websites.

Create an accurate text document with project name, project description, names of all designers and collaborators, year of creation, dimensions, materials, price, available colors, and ordering information.

NATURAL LIGHT. If you do not have a professional lighting kit or photo booth, try taking pictures outside on an overcast day. Diffused by clouds, the sun creates soft ambient light that illuminates objects without casting harsh shadows. Use a large roll or sheet of paper for a background. Smaller objects can be photographed indoors next to a window. A piece of board wrapped in aluminum foil works well as a reflector to soften dark shadows. Many images for this book were taken using this technique.

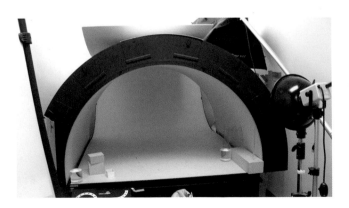

A PROFESSIONAL PHOTO BOOTH is designed for taking pictures of products with a seamless background and soft, even illumination. This type of equipment is a good investment if you photograph small objects frequently.

A PORTFOLIO IS A PRESENTATION THAT TELLS A STORY OF YOUR WORK. LEARN TO REPRESENT YOURSELF IN PRINT AND ONLINE.

SIMPLE PORTFOLIOS for letter-size pages with clear sleeves are available from most office supply stores.

Students aren't the only people who need portfolios. All independent designers need to maintain easily updated presentations of their work to show to prospective clients, employers, and business partners. Keep it clean and simple, focusing on the work. Your portfolio can be produced in various media, including printed leave-behinds, a bound book, and a website.

PRODUCT IN ACTION. Softlinks is a toddler toy consisting of colorful shapes that attach to each other in several ways. This spread from the designer's portfolio shows kids playing with the toy. The photographs dramatize and explain the product. Design: Susannah Munson, MICA.

Writing is an essential medium for promoting your work. Whether composing an email, a proposal, or a product description, take your time and be careful. Check your grammar and spelling, and always reread your work before hitting the "send" or "print" button. Writing about your product helps organize your thinking before a presentation. In your portfolio and on your website, use text and pictures together to explain your work. Writing is a creative act that, when done well, will convey the essence of your idea and express how excited you are about your product.

Talking is just as important as writing. Skype, phone calls, face-to-face meetings, and conference calls are all part of presenting your work. Meetings like these take the form of a conversation, so leave time to listen and take feedback. Be prepared for questions and criticism.

Presentation skills

Think about these questions when writing or speaking about your work:

What problem were you trying to solve?

Who is the target user?

What is the target retail price?

How will the product be used, stored, folded, washed, assembled, and disposed of?

How intuitive is its use? Will people understand how to use it and what its benefits are?

How green is your product?

How big is the market share?

What materials is it made from?

Mommy needs to apply lipstick. The flat polished area of the mommy's spoon is a handy mirror.

Emergency feeding in the car when baby spoon cannot be found.

Apply cold silver to scrapes and bruises to keep scrapes clean.

Make an instant rattling toy by adding a metal ring.

MISS MOMMY SPOON. An old silver tea spoon that belonged to my great-grandmother is still in my drawer, sitting among my stainless steel flatware. She used the spoon for its antimicrobial properties to keep water fresh in a jug, and she used it to keep hot tea from cracking glass cups by absorbing extra heat. When polished, the spoon used to send reflective sun specks jumping around our kitchen on sunny mornings. Busy moms may not have time for tea, but everyone needs a silver spoon. The Miss Mommy Spoon is practical and hardworking, not a luxury item. Design: Inna Alesina.

STEP-BY-STEP. Explain how a product is used by showing a step-by-step sequence. Combine images with clear, simple text. Like a filmmaker, use both details and distance shots to tell the story.

SOME PRODUCTS ARE DESIGNED TO TRANSFORM DURING USE. REPRESENTING YOUR PRODUCT IN SEQUENCE IS A CLEAR WAY TO SHOW CHANGE OVER TIME.

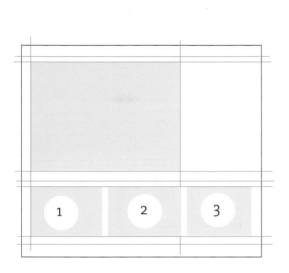

SHOWING CHANGE. This light comes as a kit of parts. The user adds items to create the finished object. Showing a sequence of steps makes it clear. Design: Inna Alesina.

COMPLEX PROCESS. This entry for a competition about dining in the year 2015 depicts a paper plate that absorbs grease and becomes translucent to reveal hidden messages. The presentation uses numbers to indicate the step-by-step transformation. Photoshop was used to clean up the paper model that we tested and photographed. Design: Inna Alesina and Sharon Zohar Gil.

1 At fast food place use Lean Plate

2 Eat slowly with food picks

3 See funny diet facts or quotes revealed as Lean Plate absorbs the grease

MARKET AND SELL

Your product's packaging, instructions, hang tags, and shipping label are all part of the overall design. Everything should communicate the benefits and attitude of your product. How an object is shipped will affect its cost and environmental impact. Try to design your product so that it folds or nests for shipping.

Think creatively about packaging. Can your product become its own packaging? Can your packaging serve as a point of purchase (POP) display? Can your packaging have an additional use after the product has been purchased?

Warehousing is another issue. Where will your inventory be stored, and how will you or other workers find its exact stock-keeping unit (SKU)? Some companies go out of business because they cannot organize their inventory efficiently at order fulfillment centers (OFCs). Packaging must be readable not only by customers but also by shippers and handlers.

How much will your product cost? Calculate your expenses for production, overhead, insurance, operations, packaging, shipping, and printed instructions. Multiply that four times to get a suggested retail price.

How will your product be sold? Imagine it on the store shelf. How will your display help explain how the product works and what its benefits are?

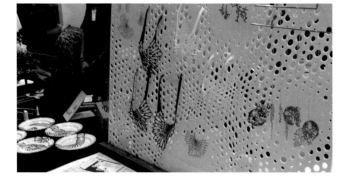

POP DISPLAY for laser-cut jewelry mirrors the production process for making the pieces. Design: Nervous System.

INFLATABLE PACKAGING protects fragile jewelry. Design: 22designstudio.

GLIMPSING THE RETAIL EXPERIENCE. These designers are selling their products at the Designboom Mart, an annual venue for designers at the ICFF in New York City.

A PRODUCT IS NOT JUST A PRODUCT. IT IS THE EMBODIMENT OF AN IDEA AND THE END RESULT OF A LONG BUT REWARDING PROCESS. MAKING A PRODUCT REAL IS AN AWESOME ADVENTURE.

Other ways designers work

Work for a studio or company. If you do not have an entrepreneurial spirit but want to learn a lot, working at a design agency can be a great start. You will be exposed to a variety of projects and learn fast. In-house designers at big companies get to see the whole picture of product development, sales, and marketing.

Be an independent freelancer. Freelance work for studios and companies can be a short exercise doing quick, fun projects, or it can become a long-term lifestyle. Sometimes, it is easier to get your foot in the door as a freelancer and later be hired as a part-time or a full-time designer.

Post your works on Coroflot. Check other portfolios on Coroflot. Contact head hunters such as Yeh IDeology or RitaSue Siegel Resources.

This chapter has outlined the steps required to take a product from the concept stage to the real world. Every project will have its own challenges. But that's why people become designers—to solve problems and create objects that people can use. The design process doesn't start or stop at the desk. All these experiences, from research to sales, make the final object better. We hope our readers will find this process rewarding and will make useful, inspiring objects of their own.

WATCH AND LISTEN. Designers often present work at trade shows to see how people react to new designs. Working in the trade booth helps designers understand what customers want. Shown here is a trade show booth at ICFF for Leaning Molds. Design: Maruja Fuentes.

ACKNOWLEDGMENTS

THANKS FROM INNA ALESINA: Never in my dreams did I think I would become an author. English is not my native language, and print is not my medium. But when Ellen Lupton suggested that the methods of experimenting with materials that I was trying with my students at MICA could be an interesting subject for a book, she brushed aside my doubts. Isn't trying out new media what I have been preaching anyway? Ellen's calm and experienced guidance and her positive attitude made it a joy to work on this book. Thank you, Ellen, for teaching and supporting me.

This book would not be a reality without the dedicated support of my students, my designer friends, and my interns, including Jackie Henisee, Olivia Peralta, Hilary Siber, and Jessica White. I also thank Ping Yang and Henry Frickel for help on models; David Trott, manager of Wegman's supermarket; and Nora Moynihan of Port Discovery Children's Museum for helping MICA students.

Very special thanks go to my husband, Leonid Guzman, for encouraging me and for helping with all the other stuff that I did not do while working on this book; to my father, Simon, and my mother-in-law, Klara, for helping with the kids; and to my sons, David, Daniel, and Elijah, for being my inspiration. And to the memory of my mother, Zinaida, who would be very proud of me.

THANKS FROM ELLEN LUPTON: When I first met Inna Alesina in 2006, I knew I wanted to work with her. Inna was an instructor at Maryland Institute College of Art, where she was applying her rigorous, hands-on design methodology to courses in our Environmental Design program. Inna also was creating brilliantly simple, original, and sustainable products, many of which I now use and enjoy every day. We decided to create this book together, bringing together our combined knowledge of contemporary design practices and our experiences as makers, educators, writers, and communicators. I'm grateful to Inna for the opportunity to work, teach, and learn with her.

This book is a project of MICA's Center for Design Thinking, which works with students and faculty at the school to develop publications, exhibitions, conferences, and other projects that contribute to the design discourse. Exploring Materials is the Center for Design Thinking's first collaboration with MICA's Environmental Design program. We are grateful to everyone at MICA for supporting the endeavor, including Gunalan Nadarajan, Vice Provost for Research; Ray Allen, Provost; Fred Lazarus, President; Mike Weikert, Director, Center for Design Practice; and Timothy Aziz, Acting Chair, Department of Environmental Design. We also thank Justin Kropp, a student in MICA's Graphic Design MFA program, for his work designing the format for this book, and MICA undergrad Julia Kostreva for creating the cover.

The editorial and production staff at Princeton Architectural Press pushed us hard to make this book readable and relevant. We are especially grateful to our editor, Clare Jacobson, who has given shape to many of my books.

Dozens of designers, students, educators, and manufacturers contributed work to this volume; our deepest thanks goes to them.

BIBLIOGRAPHY

Antonelli, Paola. *Mutant Materials in Contemporary Design*. New York: Museum of Modern Art, 1995.

Ashby, Michael. *Materials and Design: The Art and Science of Material Selection in Product Design*. Oxford: Butterworth-Heinemann, 2002.

Bell, Victoria and Patrick Rand. *Materials for Design*. New York: Princeton Architectural Press, 2006.

Bone, Martin and Kara Johnson. *I Miss My Pencil: A Design Exploration*. San Francisco: Chronicle Books, 2009.

Boylston, Scott. *Designing Sustainable Packaging*. London: Laurence King Publishing, 2009.

Brownwell, Blaine. *Transmaterial: A Catalog of Materials That Redefine Our Physical Environment*. New York: Princeton Architectural Press, 2005.

Buxton, Bill. *Sketching User Experiences: Getting the Design Right and the Right Design*. San Francisco: Morgan Kaufmann Publishers, 2007.

Cuffaro, Dan. *Process, Materials, and Measurements: All the Details Industrial Designers Need to Know but Can Never Find*. Beverly, Mass.: Rockport, 2006.

Hannah, Gail Greet. *Elements of Design: Rowena Reed Kostellow and the Structure of Visual Relationships*. New York: Princeton Architectural Press, 2002.

Kelley, Tom. *The Art of Innovation*. New York: Doubleday, 2001.

Kula, Daniel and Élodie Ternaux. *Materiology: The Creative's Guide to Materials and Technologies*. Amsterdam: Frame Publishers, 2009.

Laurel, Brenda, editor. *Design Research: Methods and Perspectives*. Cambridge, Mass.: MIT Press, 2003.

Lefteri, Chris. *Making It: Manufacturing Techniques for Product Design*. London: Laurence King, 2007.

Lesko, Jim. *Industrial Design: Materials and Manufacturing*. Hoboken, N.J.: Wiley, 1998.

___. *Materials for Inspirational Design*. East Sussex, U.K.: Rotovision, 2007.

Lidwell, William, Kristina Holden, and Jill Butler. *Universal Principles of Design*. Gloucester, Mass.: Rockport Publishers, 2003.

Lupton, Ellen. *Skin: Surface, Substance + Design*. New York: Princeton Architectural Press, 2002.

McDonough, Willliam and Michael Braungart. *Crade to Cradle: Remaking the Way We Make Things*. New York: Northpoint Press, 2002.

McQuaid, Matilda. *Extreme Textiles: Designing for High Performance*. New York: Princeton Architectural Press, 2005.

Norman, Donald. *The Design of Everyday Things*. New York: Doubleday, 1988.

Roam, Dan. *The Back of the Napkin: Solving Problems and Selling Ideas with Pictures*. New York: Penguin, 2008.

Thakara, John. *In the Bubble: Designing in a Complex World*. Cambridge, Mass.: MIT Press, 2005.

Thorpe, Ann. *The Designer's Atlas of Sustainability: Charting the Conceptual Landscape through Economy, Ecology, and Culture*. Washington, D.C.: Island Press, 2007.

INDEX